# THE TREASURE OF THE KINGDOM

*Go Buy a Field*
Matthew 13:44

## LONNIE LAWSON

LONNIE LAWSON

Printed in the United States of America
First Printing 2022
First Edition 2022

ISBN: 979-8-9873223-0-7

10 9 8 7 6 5 4 3 2 1

# THE TREASURE OF
# THE KINGDOM

# Table of Contents

# Foreword

One Sunday night after church service, I stop by a fast-food restaurant to get a burger with a friend. As we approached the front counter to place our order, we were met by a very energetic and helpful young man eagerly waiting to take our order. He asked where we had just come from all dressed up. We had just left our church services and decided to stop for something to eat. That young man at the front counter was Lonnie Lawson. Later, while we were eating, he came over to our table and asked us some questions that, he said, had been on his mind for a while about the church and the Bible. I shared a couple scriptures with him before his break was over and he went back to work. God had a purpose and a plan for our meeting that night and we all were blessed by the Word. That was the beginning of a great friendship that has lasted to this day. I adopted him as my little brother. We can talk about anything that is going on in our lives. Sometimes we talk for hours about the word of God and about life's little crooks and turns.

Over the years we have experienced many things together, both good and some not so good, but through them all, the Lord has been good. Lonnie enjoys writing and it's no wonder that he decided to write a book. The first time I heard him mention the word **Kingdom** he was so excited, and he has shared on many occasions his thoughts about God's kingdom.

He has inspired me to seek more knowledge of the kingdom. It is like he himself has been searching for something hidden for a long time and now he has possession of it. He wants to share his good fortune with this generation and the generations to come in hope that they too will find their treasure in life.

E. James Dock

A Citizen of the Kingdom of God

Shreveport, Louisiana (June 2022)

# Summary

## The Gospel that Jesus Christ Preached !

To identify as a Christian is to classify Jesus Christ as the founder of a religion called Christianity. Still, what is the point of calling Jesus Christ King if we won't treat him like the King he really is? Jesus once asked his disciples; ... *Whom do men say that I the Son of man am? Some said John, Elias, Jeremias or some other prophet. Then He asked them. "Whom say ye that I am?" Then Peter answered.... "Thou art the Christ, the Son of the living God'*. MATTHEW 16:13-18. We must worship, glorify, esteem, and honor him as King. We call Jesus Lord because earth and everything on or in the earth is the personal sovereign property belonging to the King. The domain resides on the territorial property under the dominion of a ruling King, establishing the territory as a Kingdom. Kings do not rule religions, Kings rule territories.

The story of the blind man found at the pool of Bethsaida is undoubtedly one of the most powerful testimonies of the Kingdom ever recorded; *...and they bring a blind man unto him, and besought him to touch him. And he took the blind man by the hand, and led him out of the town; and when he had spit on his eyes, and put his hands upon him, he asked him if he saw ought. And he looked up, and said, I see men as trees, walking. After that he put his hands again upon his eyes, and made him look up: and he was restored, and saw every man clearly.* MARK 8:22-25. When we see men as trees walking, or worse, when we Jesus as the founder of a religion it indicates that vision alone is not enough.

Clear vision is needed to pursue the Kingdom of God and His righteousness. God created man to influence the earth with the Kingdom of Heaven through the Kingdom of God. I encourage Apostles, Prophets, Evangelists, and Pastors. I encourage Catholics and Protestants. As well as Baptist, Pentecostals, and Televangelists, as you go preach this gospel, with the words of Jesus; *...as ye go, preach, saying, the kingdom of heaven is at hand.* MATTHEW 10:7

# Dedication

This writing is dedicated to Brenda, my wonderful wife, and a very good friend. She has always been in my corner supporting me in many ways. I feel truly gratified that God trusted me to raise and teach Brandon, David, and Shawn to become young black men in America. I never knew my biological father and I wasn't fortunate enough to always have the right mentors to teach me to be a good man. However, under the influence of the Holy Ghost, I have learned to be a good husband and a good father. Under His influence, I have worked to model my life after the righteousness of God. The Holy Spirit is more than a thrill to me. I am *LUHI*, Living Under His influence. As He helps me to write, I continue to pray for the mournful, the poor in spirit, the peacemakers, the merciful, and those who have a thirst and hunger for righteousness, that they receive the Kingdom of God. Man will come to know the joy and treasure as man discovers purpose and passion to walk in true destiny. The Lord taught me the real meaning of the expression, ***"I want to grow up to be just like my father."***

# The Kingdom of God

"Repent: for the kingdom of heaven is at hand"

☐ MATTHEW 4:17

It is my passion to share and to *"preach the Gospel that Jesus Christ Preached." ...Jesus said unto them, I must preach the kingdom of God to other cities also: for therefore am I sent.* LUKE 4:43. When God created man and commanded him to *subdue* and *have dominion*, He established His Kingdom *government* on the earth. *The earth is the Lord's, and the fullness thereof; the world, and they that dwell therein.* PSALMS 24:1. The earth is sovereign territory. The domain is established on the territory. The dominion is the established order over the domain. The earth is the sovereign property which belongs to the Lord who is King, establishing the domain to be a Kingdom. The word *"Lord"* appears over 2400 times in the bible text, demonstrating ownership. This is why we affirm *"Jesus is Lord!"*. Having been born in democracy and raised in religion we the people need to understand that the Kingdom of God is *"not"* a republic. The Kingdom of God is *"not"* a religion. Jesus Christ never identified with any traditional system of religion of his day. Jesus is the King who never preached democracy or religion. God's priority for man in the earth has always been dominion, never religion nor religious liberties. Religion is the jet plane circling the airport that never comes in for a landing. Jesus taught *...as ye go, preach, saying, the kingdom of heaven is at hand.* MATTHEW 10:7.

*God said, "Let Us make man in Our image, according to Our likeness; let them have dominion over the fish of the sea, over the birds of the air, and over the cattle, over all the earth and over every creeping thing that creeps on the earth". ...Then God blessed them, and God said to them, "Be fruitful and multiply; fill the earth and subdue it; have dominion over the fish of the sea, over the birds of the air, and over every living thing that moves on the earth".* GENESIS-1:26-28.

The lexicon or vernacular of the bible is that of a King and his Kingdom. Whether the words are Greek, Hebrew or Arabic. Whether the translation is Latin, Spanish, French, or English; the language, the context, and the lexis can be identified as the language of a King. The Genesis story uses words such as *dominion, subdue*, and *rule;* these words do not signify religion; however, they do identify government. The Kingdom of God will establish righteousness and order. Religion is too abstract and subject to the perception of men to maintain such structure and order. In the absence of Kingdom of Heaven influence men are left to anarchy *...there was no king in Israel, but every man did that which was right in his own eyes.* JUDGES 17:6. Jesus preached *...as ye go, preach, saying, the kingdom of heaven is at hand.* MATTHEW 10:7.

In the beginning the Holy Spirit, the first person to arrive, brought order and structure to the earth that was dark, void, and without form. In the Genesis story God said let there be light and the sun became the center of the solar system bringing light, warmth, and energy. God spoke again and the atmosphere was divided into the troposphere, the stratosphere, the mesosphere, the thermosphere and the exosphere. God said that the earth should bring forth grasses and trees. The grasses and trees should bring forth herbs and fruit. The fruit should bring forth seed that produces after its own kind. The skies and seas were filled with birds and fish that produce after their kind. The cattle and four-legged beast were filled with seed to produce after their own kind. Religion is too abstract to create such order.

The priority of the Holy Spirit is to administer the will of the King over the territory. The Kingdom of God is the influence of the Kingdom of Heaven on the earth. The priority of the Holy Spirit is to teach the will, the values, the ethics, and the culture of the King, so that the citizens begin to *talk* like the King, *walk* like the King, *live* just like the King. God wants the influence of the Kingdom of Heaven to extend to the earth through the Kingdom of God. *... Thy kingdom come, thy will be done in earth, as it is in heaven...* MATTHEW 6:10. We must pursue kingdom life and righteousness. *Seek ye first the kingdom of God and His righteousness* MATTHEW 6:33. God created man to think like a King, *"...after mine own heart..."* ACTS 13:22. God has provisioned resource, peace, well-being, and security in an environment designed specifically for the man. Man is expected to rule with integrity, efficiency, righteousness, peace, and joy.

As the King establishes His dominion over the territory the King will *put* a governor in place fortified with His influence to make sure that the values and culture of His Kingdom are demonstrated in the distant territory. God prepared a place for the man and there, God put the man. The man was put in the presence of God to govern all things created in the earth. God gave mankind a mandate, to have dominion, to subdue, and to rule. God fortified mankind with His spirit, and then the man was reinforced with a sound mind and sense of well-being; *God blessed them!* Think for a moment, only an even-tempered well adjusted, mentally, and emotionally secure man will be trusted to rule according to the righteousness of God. He was released to fill the earth with the nature, and the influence of God.

There was a good reason why Abram had to disengage from his home country. God separated Abram from his father and his country to separate him from his old system of living. *Lift your eyes now and look from the place where you are...; for all the land which you see I give to you and your descendants forever.* GENESIS 13:14-15. God showed Abram a territory filled with people living by their own set of ideas, philosophies, and concepts. *... The Kenites, and the Kenizzites, and the Kadmonites, and the Hittites, and the Perizzites, and the Rephaims, and the Amorites, and the Canaanites, and the Girgashites, and the Jebusites.* GENESIS 15:19. God then gave Abram and the nation His own ideas, culture, values, ethics, and disciplines. *You shall not bow down to their gods, nor serve them, nor do according to their works;* EXODUS 23:24. God restricted

Abraham from adopting the cultures in the territory with the expressed purpose to bring the territory under the influence of the Kingdom of God; the kingdom of heaven has arrived. God used Abraham to birth a nation, Joseph to preserve the nation, Moses to deliver the nation. God used Joshua to forge the nation. David was used to rule the nation. God sent His son, Jesus, to die and redeem the nation. The Apostles came to disciple the nations. Religion was never the priority of these men.

The most powerful relationship in the Kingdom is the one between the father and the son. Adam, the son created in the image of God and *put* in power. Adam was the ***manifest idea of God. ...the Lord God formed every beast of the field, and every fowl of the air; and brought them unto Adam to see what he would call them: and whatsoever Adam called every living creature that was the name thereof.*** GENESIS 2:19. Adam spoke to creation, whatever Adam called them that was the name thereof. Although Adam had enormous power and unfettered access, he was persuaded by the prince of darkness that God could not be trusted. ***...the serpent said to the woman, "You will not surely die. For God knows that in the day you eat of it your eyes will be opened and you will be like God, knowing good and evil."*** GENESIS 3:1-5. Giving birth to an adversarial relationship between The King and the son. ***So, he drove out the man; and he placed at the east of the garden of Eden Cherubims, and a flaming sword which turned every way, to keep the way of the tree of life.*** GENESIS 3:24. Adam lost his identity, making him the first victim of identity theft. The governing system was hijacked by a rogue agent, the prince of darkness. Not only did the thieving cherub want to steal man's identity, he wanted to assume it as well. Adam abdicated authority invested in him and forfeited it to the ***prince of darkness,*** leaving the control of the world to an illegal, illegitimate, counterfeit control. The father of all lies proceeded to establish his counterfeit control of the world systems. Adam became disobedient and driven from the presence of God. As time passed the wickedness of man became great in the earth, and every intent of his heart made man lose sight of the priority of God, ***dominion over the earth.***

The spirit of discord is manifested in many different ways around the world. We know it as civil disobedience, protest, rioting, racial or social injustice, and police brutality. The bible refers to it as **enmity**. No matter what we call it, it is designed to undermine our fellowship with the Father. Adam committed an act of treason and disobedience, declared independence violating a boundary set by the Creator. God built a wall because man couldn't be trusted to respect God's righteousness. God *placed at the east of the garden of Eden Cherubims, and a flaming sword which turned every way, to keep the way of the tree of life.* GENESIS 3:24.

*Why do the heathen rage, and the people imagine a vain thing? The kings of the earth set themselves, and the rulers take counsel together, against the Lord and against His Anointed, saying, let us break their bonds in pieces and cast away their cords from us. He who sits in the heavens shall laugh;* PSALMS 2:1-5.

The people have done a vain thing. The rulers of the earth have perverted God's *idea* of dominion to mean human abuse, exploitation, and domination. Human inspired governments differ from the Kingdom of God in terms of precepts, ideologies, and concepts. No human empire, dynasty, democracy or republic will compare to the Kingdom of God and His righteousness. Dictators and tyrants are only happy in paranoia, psychosis, and narcissism, and at the core of that vanity is a crippling insecurity. A hodgepodge of narcissistic murderers who only want to satisfy their own lust are in control of world governments. Their psychosis makes life insecure and anxious, a long way from green pastures and still waters. There is a longstanding debate about which government is best for mankind. From empires, to dynasties, to democracies to republics, man will not be able to depend on any of them. It will not matter who is in control, the oligarch, the despot, the tyrant, or the socialist, all of them will fail. The kings of the earth have cut themselves off from the Lord and have decided not to follow his mandate for government. Human governments refuse to model God's righteousness, integrity, influence, glory, justice, structure, and legitimacy.

Jesus was the only begotten son. Jesus was conceived and vested with power. Jesus was validated by his Father and he was obedient unto death. Jesus is the Christ. Jesus is the *expressed idea of God. In the beginning was the Word, and the Word was with God, and the Word was God. The same was in the beginning with God. All things were made by him; and without him was not anything made that was made.* JOHN 1:1-3. Jesus speaks to create. Jesus is the word made flesh, the expressed conceived ideas of God. Jesus once asked his disciples; ... *Whom do men say that I the Son of man am? Some said John, Elias, Jeremias or some other prophet. Then He asked them. "Whom say ye that I am?" Then Peter answered.... "Thou art the Christ, the Son of the living God'.* MATTHEW 16:13-18. The legitimate, legal, indisputable, anointed King. He came to reestablish his government authorizing his *ekklesia,* the well-defined assembly of citizens belonging to Christ, to influence the earth. This is why we call Jesus *Lord; ...a child is born and a son is given and the government shall be upon his shoulder; and his name shall be called Wonderful, Counselor, The mighty God, The everlasting Father, The Prince of Peace"* ISAIAH 9:6.

Jesus is classically misunderstood. According to one bible story the parents of Jesus had traveled from Jerusalem to Nazareth a full day's journey before they noticed that they had forgotten Jesus. When they finally found him, they were *"astonished"* to find the twelve-year-old sitting, listening, exchanging ideas, and asking questions with teachers and doctors. Jesus replied to them; " *Why did you seek Me? Did you not know that I must be about My Father's business?"* LUKE 2:49. The reply confused his parents because they didn't seem to understand and forgot why the child was born. During his time in Judea Jesus had to contend with the clash of two illegitimate systems. Pilate needed to protect Roman control while the Pharisees needed to protect religious control. Making Jesus the target of a schizophrenic system of government and religion. Jesus was increasingly popular with the people living in the territory and the religious were intimidated. The Pharisees were no match for the influence of Jesus, and they wanted to put a stop to it. Pilate and the religious had one common motivation, put a stop to the authority of Jesus, the King.

Jesus is classically misunderstood by the Humanists, Atheists, and the Gnostics. The Jews, Muslims nor Christians understand him any better. We have reduced Him to a religious leader. Jesus is not a failed prophet nor is he the founder of any religion. What is the point of calling Jesus King if we won't regard him as the King that He is? Jesus begins preaching and teaching in Judea, a territory under Judeo Greek influence and Roman occupation. From the beginning of His ministry and for the next three years we can identify the priority of Jesus. To preach the Kingdom of God. Remember Jesus never preached democracy or religion. Jesus came to establish his *ekklesia* to manage and administer the will of the King on the earth. Jesus is King.

John the Baptist came preaching in the wilderness of Judea. It was prophesied that John would prepare the way of the Lord. *In those days came John the Baptist, preaching in the wilderness of Judaea, and saying, Repent ye: for the kingdom of heaven is at hand.* MATTHEW 3:1-2. Jesus was baptized of John, to identify with the master teacher and his school of thought. Jesus and other master teachers of his time often used language from the school of psychology, words such as teach, preach, believe, hear, persuade, heart, even the word repent, all from the Kingdom school of thought. *"Repent, for the kingdom of heaven is at hand."* MATTHEW 4:17.

Jesus came to the hood *... the Word became flesh and dwelt among us, and we beheld His glory, the glory as of the only begotten of the Father, full of grace and truth.* JOHN 1:14. Jesus came to earth to retrieve His system and re-establish His Kingdom on the earth. One day Jesus stood in the synagogue and read from the book of the prophet Esaias. *... The Spirit of the Lord is upon me, because he hath anointed me to preach the gospel to the poor; he hath sent me to heal the brokenhearted, to preach deliverance to the captives, and recovering of sight to the blind, to set at liberty them that are bruised, to preach the acceptable year of the Lord. And he closed the book, and he gave it again to the minister, and sat down. ...And he began to say unto them, this day is this scripture fulfilled in your ears.* LUKE 4:17-21

*...And he said unto them, I must preach the kingdom of God to other cities also: for therefore am I sent.* LUKE 4:43.

Words are expressed conceived ideas, from precept to concept. Jesus is the word made flesh, making Jesus the **expressed** idea of God. *In the beginning was the Word, and the Word was with God, and the Word was God. The same was in the beginning with God. All things were made by him; and without him was not anything made that was made.* JOHN 1:1-3. Jesus was also identified as the master teacher, or rabbi in the New Testament. The men who followed the master teacher were identified as disciples, learning the disciplines taught by the master rabbi. There are 27 books in the KJV New Testament. There are four recorded accounts of the three years Jesus taught disciples. There is one historical book annotating the Acts of the Apostles. There are 22 epistles explaining the Kingdom of God and the sacrifice of Jesus, 14 of those were written by Paul alone. So much is written to teach and to explain you will be right to conclude that it is more powerful to think like God and not just follow the signs. If religious people stop focusing so much on how Jesus performed and focused more on what Jesus taught, the church wouldn't appear to be so impotent. *And he said unto them, go ye into all the world, and preach the gospel to every creature. He that believeth and is baptized shall be saved; but he that believeth not shall be damned. And these signs shall follow them that believe;* MARK 16:15-18.

Jesus, who is King, spent three years teaching and preaching the Kingdom of God. As Jesus preached, he challenged us to change our way of thinking; *"for the kingdom of heaven has arrived"*. A kingdom is a domain ruled and governed by a king. Our priority is to manifest the invisible Kingdom of Heaven, extending the influence of the King to the earth through the Kingdom of God.

Jesus established his ekklesia and commissioned them to go into; ...*And he said unto them, go ye into all the world, and preach the gospel to every creature.* MARK 16:15. Jesus taught the disciples to pray *Thy kingdom come. Thy will be done in earth, as it is in heaven...*MATTHEW 6:10 The ekklesia has been fortified with the Holy Spirit, to go to all the world systems with kingdom influence. We, like yeast, must go into the loaf *...The kingdom of heaven is like unto leaven, which a woman took, and hid in three measures of meal, till the whole was leavened.* MATTHEW 13:33. Adam was never mandated to start a religion; *Then God said, ...let them have dominion ...over all the earth...be fruitful and multiply; fill the earth and subdue it;* GENESIS 1:26-28.

The priority of the democratic republic is personal and religious liberties. *"We hold these truths to be self-evident, that all men are created equal, that they are endowed by their Creator with certain unalienable rights, that among these are life, liberty, and the pursuit of happiness."* –DECLARATION OF INDEPENDENCE. The democratic republic teaches men to pursue individual happiness, religious and personal liberties. *...every man is tempted, when he is drawn away of his own lust,* JAMES 1:14. There will be no guarantee of kingdom righteousness if every man is allowed to follow his own perception of individual or religious rights. The Kingdom of God is not the same as the democratic republic. Jesus never taught democracy. Jesus taught Kingdom. *Repent, for the kingdom of heaven is at hand* MATTHEW 4:17. Jesus begins his ministry preaching kingdom. Jesus spends three years teaching his disciples about the virtues of the Kingdom of Heaven and demonstrating how the government of His Kingdom works. The Kingdom and the church that will manifest the will, the values, and the culture of the king in the earth. The church will take back territory and His kingdom influence will increase. *For the kingdom of God is not meat and drink; but righteousness, and peace, and joy in the Holy Ghost.* ROMANS 14:17

There is no human government to compare to the Kingdom of God. The Lord knows that the rulers of the earth will abuse you. The rulers will exploit you, and those you love. *He will take your sons, and appoint them for himself, for his chariots, and to be his horsemen; and some shall run before his chariots. And he will appoint him captains over thousands, and captains over fifties; and will set them to ear his ground, and to reap his harvest, and to make his instruments of war, and instruments of his chariots. And he will take your daughters to be confectionaries, and to be cooks, and to be bakers. And he will take your fields, and your vineyards, and your olive yards, even the best of them, and give them to his servants. And he will take the tenth of your seed, and of your vineyards, and give to his officers, and to his servants. And he will take your menservants, and your maidservants, and your goodliest young men, and your asses, and put them to his work. He will take the tenth of your sheep: and ye shall be his servants.* 1 SAMUEL 8:11-17. The rulers of the earth will take from you and give to his friends. The Lord knows that these men have no integrity, and they want to live in abundance and luxury while the citizens languish. The tyrant will have no interest in the wellbeing of the people. The despot will use his power to abuse and exploit the people while he enriches his own life. We can never look to tyrants, despots, or dictators for our well-being. You will be forced to fight his wars and to make his weapons of war and equipment. The rulers of the earth will be oppressive, wasteful, and exploitive.

We need to change our way of thinking. We need to stop asserting our narrative and allow the Holy Spirit to reveal Kingdom truth. We should begin with proper exegetical review of scripture. Starting with the word *repent.* The word repent is not a call for remorse. The word repent is from the school of psychology, *from the Greek metanoia-after thought, from metanoein-to change one's mind or purpose, from meta-indicating change or noein, to have mental perception, from noose-mind and thought. -* ONLINE ETYMOLOGY DICTIONARY. Though the word may suggest sorrow and regret, it is significantly more. In other words, change our way of thinking, the kingdom of heaven has arrived.

Jesus began his ministry teaching; *"Repent, for the kingdom of heaven is at hand"* MATTHEW4:17. The word repent is not a call to remorse. In the King James Version of the Bible, its verbal cognate is translated as repent. Men are challenged by Jesus to a personal, absolute surrender to God as Sovereign. *"Repent, for the kingdom of heaven is at hand"* is the Jesus way of telling us that we are on the wrong train, following the wrong breadcrumbs, headed in the wrong direction. We need to stop walking after the counsel of the ungodly, PSALMS 1:1. We should get off the train that leads us to bad ideas, concepts, principles, convictions, and ethics. We need to make reservations on the kingdom train of thought. We need to change our priorities to *seek the kingdom of God, and his righteousness first.* Change our way of thinking to change our way of living. ***Therefore, if any man be in Christ, he is a new creature: old things are passed away; behold, all things are become new.*** 2 CORINTHIANS 5:17

The kingdom is the liberation for the persecuted, the oppressed, and the victimized. MATTHEW 5:2-10. Jesus once said that the kingdom is like a treasure. ***...the kingdom of heaven is like treasure hidden in a field, which a man found and hid; and for joy over it he goes and sells all that he has and buys that field.*** MATTHEW 13:44. When men discover the treasure in the Kingdom of God, they will give up all they know to gain access to the Kingdom. Man was created to live with a legitimate efficient government of great integrity where wealth, justice, and peace are common. The fifth chapter of New Testament Matthew goes further to voice the antithesis of Jesus. Straight from the voice of the King, the Son of God we hear and learn what the religious has never understood regarding Jesus or the laws of His kingdom. The summary of that voice can be found in MATTHEW 5:21-42.

*The kingdom of heaven is like to a grain of mustard seed, which a man took, and sowed in his field: Which indeed is the least of all seeds: but when it is grown, it is the greatest among herbs, and becomes a tree, so that the birds of the air come and lodge in the branches thereof.* MATTHEW 13:31-32.

*Again, the kingdom of heaven is like unto a merchant man, seeking goodly pearls: who, when he had found one pearl of great price, went, and sold all that he had, and bought it.* MATTHEW 13:45

*Again, the kingdom of heaven is like unto a net, that was cast into the sea, and gathered of every kind:* MATTHEW 13:47

I was born in the democratic republic and raised in religion. However, I've learned that Jesus never preached democracy, nor did Jesus establish any religion. Jesus established his *ekklesia*. I have further learned that the Kingdom of God is neither a religion nor a republic. I also learned that Jesus did not personally deliver the constitution of the republic to Thomas Jefferson. I had to acknowledge that there were religious and political concepts I needed to unlearn. I am encouraged to preach the gospel that Jesus Christ preached. *The disciple is not above his master: but every one that is perfect shall be as his master. ...why call ye me, Lord, Lord, and do not the things which I say? Whosoever cometh to me, and heareth my sayings, and doeth them, ... is like a man which built a house, and digged deep, and laid the foundation on a rock: and when the flood arose, the stream beat vehemently upon that house, and could not shake it: for it was founded upon a rock.* LUKE 6:40-49. Jesus established his *ekklesia*. *...And he said unto them, I must preach the kingdom of God to other cities also: for therefore am I sent.* LUKE 4:43. The pursuit of Kingdom living and lifestyle has become my priority and my passion. As I was growing up, I was taught that it is not possible to know the mind of God. However, if I held to that belief, how could I explain God's testimony concerning David; *...I have found David the son of Jesse, a man after My own heart, who will do all My will.* ACTS 13:21-22. Peace came to me after I read 1st Corinthians chapter two. In this writing Paul takes care to help us understand the difference between carnal thinking and spiritual thinking. To the carnal mind the things of God are mysterious. Some might say they are even foolishness. The carnal mind will think it was foolishness to send frogs, flies, and locusts to overthrow an oppressor. The carnal mind will think it was foolishness to send 300 men instead of 32,000 to face down an aggressive enemy. The carnal mind will think it was foolishness for Christ to die for the ungodly. *God hath revealed them unto us by his Spirit: for the Spirit searcheth all things, yea, the deep things of God. For what man knoweth the things of a man, save the spirit of man which is in him? even so the things of God knoweth no man, but the Spirit of God. Now we have received, not the spirit of the world, but the spirit which is of God; that we might know the things that are freely given to us of God. ...For who hath known the mind of the Lord, that he may* *instruct him? But we have the mind of Christ.* 1 CORINTHIANS We need to build our house on the sure foundation of ideas and concepts that pursue the Kingdom of Heaven, we need the mind of Christ.

Satan is called the prince of darkness for a reason; *...The god of this world hath blinded the minds of them which believe not, lest the light of the glorious gospel of Christ, who is the image of God, should shine unto them.* 2 CORINTHIANS 4:2. Satan will always target us with subtle disinformation and deception.

We have forgotten the Adam that God created. It is as if we can't remember Genesis chapters one and two, as we only share the story from Genesis chapter three. Man was created with the capacity of thought. *For God has not given us a spirit of fear, but of power and of love and of a sound mind* 2 TIMOTHY 1:7. Adam was given access to every resource in creation. He was also given a boundary, a restriction. Adam was then given a choice; will he choose life or will he choose death? Will God be able to trust that the man will respect the boundary and make the correct decision? One day Adam made a very unfortunate decision. One solitary act of treasonous disobedience changed everything for all mankind. Now all men have to live with the bad decision of one man, *...by one-man sin entered into the world, and death by sin; and so, death passed upon all men, for that all have sinned: ...by the offence of one judgment came upon all men to condemnation;* ROMANS 5:18-19

After the resurrection, the disciples were commissioned...*And he said unto them, go ye into all the world, and preach the gospel to every creature.* MARK 16:15. The ekklesia has a mandate to go to all the world systems with kingdom influence. The world systems: economics, healthcare, education, entertainment, sports, eco, and political systems are to be influenced by the King of God; *Thy kingdom come. Thy will be done in earth, as it is in heaven...* MATTHEW 6:10 The ekklesia, fortified with God the Holy Spirit, will impact the territory and His government will increase. *Of the increase of His government and peace there will be no end....* ISAIAH 9:7

*...the kingdom of heaven is like unto a man that is an householder, which bringeth forth out of his treasure things new and old.* MATTHEW 13:52

*And he cometh to Bethsaida; and they bring a blind man unto him, and besought him to touch him. And he took the blind man by the hand, and led him out of the town; and when he had spit on his eyes, and put his hands upon him, he asked him if he saw ought. And he looked up, and said, I see men as trees, walking. After that he put his hands again upon his eyes and made him look up: and he was restored, and saw every man clearly.* MARK 8:22-25

*...there was no king in Israel, but every man did that which was right in his own eyes.* JUDGES 17:6.

Imagine that you are on the train of thought departing from the place of divine *ideas*. You will find bread crumbs; *image, conviction, principles, ethics, values, teaching, disciplines,* and *beliefs,* with stops at *ideology, philosophy, concepts, and psychology,* leading you to the place of divine destiny, *saintly system of living.* The place where all men are equal, righteousness, peace, and joy in the Holy Ghost are priority, and the pursuit of the Kingdom is happiness. *"We are not human beings having a spiritual experience; we are spiritual beings having a human experience." --Pierre Teilhard de Chardin.* Having been born in democracy and raised in religion there are many concepts that we need to unlearn. This may prove to be a challenge because religious people are not given to critical thinking. They believe that critical thinking is an attack on their faith. If your faith is threatened by your carnal thinking consider this; *Beloved, believe not every spirit, but try the spirits whether they are of God: because many false prophets are gone out into the world.* 1 JOHN 4:1. When you hear from other spirits and other gods, trust me you will, you need to verify every word using the Holy Ghost as your divine critical thinking filter.

*He breathed on them, and said to them, Receive the Holy Spirit.* JOHN 20:22. The Kingdom will make an impact with the will, the values, the culture, and the language of the King. Christ empowered the twelve disciples with the Holy Ghost and authorized them to impact the earth through the Kingdom of God. Man is expected to rule with integrity, influence, efficiency, righteousness, peace, and joy. *And as ye go, preach, saying, the kingdom of heaven is at hand.* MATTHEW 10:7

*"Preach the Gospel that Jesus Christ Preached." -Dr. Myles Monroe.*

# The Kingdom Bill of Rights!

"Repent, for the kingdom of heaven is at hand

☐ MATTHEW 4:17

Jesus begins his ministry preaching about the kingdom. Jesus spends the next three years teaching his disciples about the kingdom of heaven and explaining how the government of His kingdom works.

*...Then He opened His mouth and taught them, saying:*

- *Blessed are the poor in spirit, for theirs is the kingdom of heaven.*

- *Blessed are those who mourn, for they shall be comforted.*

- *Blessed are the meek, for they shall inherit the earth.*

- *Blessed are those who hunger and thirst for righteousness, for they shall be filled.*

- *Blessed are the merciful, for they shall obtain mercy.*

- *Blessed are the pure in heart, for they shall see God.*

- *Blessed are the peacemakers, for they shall be called sons of God.*

- *Blessed are those who are persecuted for righteousness' sake, for theirs is the kingdom of heaven.*

- *Blessed are you when they revile and persecute you, and say all kinds of evil against you falsely for My sake.*

- *Rejoice and be exceedingly glad, for great is your reward in heaven, for so they persecuted the prophets who were before you.* MATTHEW 5:2-10

# Kingdom Antithesis

Pay No Attention to The Man Behind the Curtain

☐ MATTHEW 5:17

Adam, trying to satisfy a thirst and a hunger, followed the yellow brick road to Emerald City. A place full of illusion and a big booming voice shrouded in fire and smoke only to become a victim of lying dysfunctional men hiding behind curtains pulling levers and pushing buttons. Men who pledged to be advocates of individual rights on one hand, while on the other, allow human beings to be commoditized and reduced to property. Masquerading as powerful champions often regarded as deeply religious and ethically minded men who desired to treat all men justly. The rulers of the earth work against the Lord and His anointed and they have perverted God's *idea* of dominion to express and establish human domination. Human governments are antithetic to the Kingdom of Heaven in terms of priority, justice, integrity, influence, legitimacy, efficiency, and righteousness. *The kings of the earth set themselves, and the rulers take counsel together, against the Lord and against His Anointed, saying, let us break their bonds in pieces and cast away their cords from us...; PSALMS 2:1-5.*

A hodgepodge of psychotic murderers who only want to satisfy their own lust are in control of world governments. Dictators and tyrants are narcissistic, and paranoid. At the core of that vanity is a crippling insecurity. The capitalist, the despot, the tyrant, and the socialist will stumble and fall. The kings of the earth have cut themselves off from the Lord and have decided not to follow his model for government.

Human domination is a threat to sovereign creative ownership rights and will only steal, kill, and destroy.

The Lord knows that the rulers of the earth will not follow His righteousness. Human governments have been abusive and malevolent. Listen to cable news to hear about all types of atrocities committed by men who show no respect or regard for the citizens who live under their rule. Is it any wonder that men don't trust governments? Immoral and unethical leaders have created an echo of disillusion that can be heard around the world. From Egypt to Syria to Russia to America, men are unhappy and angry with human government.

*This will be the behavior of the king who will reign over you: He will take your sons and appoint them for his own chariots and to be his horsemen, and some will run before his chariots... He will take your daughters to be perfumers, cooks, and bakers. And he will take the best of your fields, your vineyards, and your olive groves... And he will take your male servants, your female servants, your finest young men, and your donkeys, and put them to his work. He will take a tenth of your sheep. And you will be his servants. And you will cry out in that day because of your king whom you have chosen for yourselves, and the Lord will not hear you in that day.* 1 SAMUEL 8:11-17. The Lord knows that the rulers of the earth will abuse you. The rulers will exploit you, those you love, and all your resources. The rulers of the earth will take from you and give to his partners in crime. The Lord knows that the men have no integrity and they want to live in abundance and luxury while the citizens languish. The tyrant will have no interest in the wellbeing of the people. The despot will use his power to abuse and exploit the people while he enriches his own life. We can never look to tyrants, despots, or dictators for our well-being. Stop expecting them to do the just and righteous thing.

I grew up hearing that the Lord moves in mysterious ways. However, as I grew up in the Lord, I began to understand that God's ways are not as mysterious as they are antithetical. "*For my thoughts are not your thoughts, neither are your ways my ways*" .... ISAIAH 55:8. Jesus was often time heard saying; *The kingdom of heaven is like.*

Antithesis:

- A person or thing that is the direct opposite of someone or something else. *"love is the antithesis of selfishness."*
- The rhetorical contrast of ideas by means of parallel arrangements of words, clauses, or sentences. *"they promised freedom and provided slavery".*
- A figure of speech in which an opposition or contrast of ideas is expressed by parallelism of words that are opposites. *"hatred stirs up strife, but love covers all sins."*

*...and they bring a blind man unto him, and besought him to touch him. And he took the blind man by the hand, and led him out of the town; and when he had spit on his eyes, and put his hands upon him, he asked him if he saw ought. And he looked up, and said, I see men as trees, walking. After that he put his hands again upon his eyes, and made him look up: and he was restored, and saw every man clearly.* MARK 8:22-25. All religions start in psychologies driven by philosophies born in ideologies creating a personal system of living. Jesus touched the blind man to secure his sight. It appeared that the man did regain his sight but his perception distorted his vision. Jesus touched the man again to secure clear vision with his recovered sight. There was a good reason why God advised Abraham to never walk after the Perizzites, Jebusites, Canaanites or any of the other people already in Canaan. God wanted His nation to follow His ideas, culture, and his righteousness. God restricted Abraham from adopting the ideologies in the territory with the expressed purpose to bring the territory under the influence of the Kingdom of God. *You shall not bow down to their gods, nor serve them, nor do according to their works;* EXODUS 23:24.; *the kingdom of heaven has arrived.* To pursue the Kingdom of God and His righteousness, we need the Antithesis of Jesus.

The Antithesis of Jesus is of considerable significance. To pursue the Kingdom of God and His righteousness, we need the mind of Christ. *Think not that I am come to destroy the law, or the prophets: I am not come to destroy, but to fulfil.* MATTHEW 5:17. *Seek ye first the kingdom of God and His righteousness* MATTHEW 6:33. Who better to teach, demonstrate, and help us to understand His righteousness than Jesus himself? The Antithesis of Jesus indicates that Jesus did not teach democracy nor did he establish religion. The well-known quote of Jesus *"I am not come to destroy the law, but to fulfil"* was declared at the time when Jesus began to preach and teach Kingdom.

Judea was occupied by Rome. Caesar had put Pilate in position to make the citizens of Judea follow Roman law. As we pursue the kingdom of God and His righteousness, we need of hear His thoughts and learn His ways. Jesus authored His law, and no one will understand His law better. No one will be more qualified teaching and revealing His law and His righteousness. I read somewhere that Jesus is the most misunderstood person on earth. If that is truly the case then we need to hear the thoughts and learn the ways of Jesus. Jesus never identified with the religious Pharisees. Jesus was baptized by John in the wilderness. Jesus identifies with John, preaching in the wilderness. *Repent ye: for the kingdom of heaven is at hand.* MATTHEW 3:2. I want to identify with Jesus. Baptized in the name of the Father, Son, and Holy Ghost.

*In the beginning was the Word, and the Word was with God, and the Word was God. The same was in the beginning with God. All things were made by him; and without him was not anything made that was made. In him was life; and the life was the light of men. And the light shineth in darkness; and the darkness comprehended it not ... The same came for a witness, to bear witness of the Light, that all men through him might believe.* JOHN 1:1-7. Jesus, our Master Teacher, will give us His *light* so we can have a full and complete understanding of His righteousness and His life. *...we have received, not the spirit of the world, but the spirit which is of God; that we might know the things that are freely given to us of God. ...For who hath known the mind of the Lord, that he may instruct him? But we have the mind of Christ.* 1 CORINTHIANS 2:10. Jesus makes his announcement; *Repent, for the kingdom of heaven is at hand.* MATTHEW 4:17

Now consider the Antithesis of Jesus.

- *For I say unto you, that except your righteousness shall exceed the righteousness of the scribes and Pharisees, ye shall in no case enter into the kingdom of heaven.* MATTHEW 5:20.

The righteousness of the scribes and Pharisees is not His righteousness. Tyrants, despots, and dictators will pull the religion lever to validate domination, false gods and prop up illegitimate domains. Religious men want escapism along with a collection of pagan rituals, and superstitions. Religion is the house of mirrors filled with distorted reflections that only lead to U-turns, turn arounds, and dead ends. *You shall not bow down to their gods, nor serve them, nor do according to their works;* EXODUS 23:24. God restricted Abraham from adopting the strange cultures with the expressed purpose to bring the territory under the influence of the Kingdom of God. It is important to understand that the Kingdom of God is neither a religion nor a republic.

- *Ye have heard that it was said by them of old time, thou shalt not kill; and whosoever shall kill shall be in danger of the judgment:*
  - *...But I say unto you, that whosoever is angry with his brother without a cause shall be in danger of the judgment:* MATTHEW 5:21-26.

Anger is the seed that yields the fruit of murder. When anger is enough to conceive death, murder will be manifested, to which there will be consequence. A good reason why anger and bitterness should never be allowed to fester. If you nurture anger and bitterness you will give way to murder. *Thou shalt love thy neighbor as thyself...*MATTHEW 22:35-40.

- *It hath been said, whosoever shall put away his wife, let him give her a writing of divorcement:*
  - *...But I say unto you, that whosoever shall put away his wife, saving for the cause of fornication, causes her to commit adultery: and whosoever shall marry her that is divorced committed adultery.* MATTHEW 5:31-32.

The very first human contract was certified in Genesis, *therefore shall a man leave his father and his mother and shall cleave unto his wife: and they shall be one flesh.* GENESIS 2:23-25. Everything established under this contract is legitimate, lawful and valid. The integrity of the parties of the contract will safeguard the honor of the agreement. Adultery is the voluntary violation that destroys the integrity of the contract. God is the God of great integrity and he will protect his word to protect his name. *...I will sanctify my great name, ...which was profaned among the heathen, which ye have profaned in the midst of them; ...the heathen shall know that I am the Lord, ...Not for your sakes do I this, saith the Lord God. ... But for mine holy name's sake.* EZEKIEL 36:22-26; 32. After all if you can't be trusted to honor a contract with man how will you honor your covenant with God? *Thou shalt love thy neighbor as thyself...*MATTHEW 22:35-40.

- *Again, you have heard that it was said to those of old, you shall not swear falsely, but shall perform your oaths to the Lord.*

o *...But I say to you, do not swear at all: neither by heaven, for it is God's throne; nor by the earth, for it is His footstool; nor by Jerusalem, for it is the city of the great King. Nor shall you swear by your head, because you cannot make one hair white or black. But let your Yes be Yes, and your No, No. For whatever is more than these is from the evil one.* MATTHEW 5:33-37.

In the Genesis story satan launched an attack on the integrity of God. An attempt to persuade man that God can't be trusted. Integrity is a priority in the Kingdom. As we pursue the Kingdom, we must pursue with integrity. Men with integrity don't have to swear to anything. Never make promises you can't or won't keep. Never promise bread only to give a stone. Don't promise fish only to give a serpent. Don't be a fraud or a trickster. God's integrity is not up for sale. His integrity is whole, complete, and full. Isn't it great to have a King whom you can trust without fail? *The fear of man brings a snare, but whoever trusts in the Lord shall be safe.* PROVERBS 29:25.

- *You have heard that it was said, An eye for an eye and a tooth for a tooth.*
  - *...But I tell you not to resist an evil person. But whoever slaps you on your right cheek, turn the other to him also. If anyone wants to sue you and take away your tunic, let him have your cloak also. And whoever compels you to go one mile, go with him two. Give to him who asks you, and from him who wants to borrow from you do not turn away.* MATTHEW 5:38-42

Righteousness will demand justice. *...For the kingdom of God is not meat and drink; but righteousness, and peace, and joy in the Holy Ghost.* ROMANS 14:17. *"No Justice No Peace!* Righteousness demands justice and man will have no joy or peace until righteousness has been requited. However, when man tries to get justice it is not justice it's revenge. As we pursue His Kingdom and His righteousness, we pursue His justice. In the Kingdom Bill of Rights Jesus has promised his justice in the Kingdom. *Blessed are those who hunger and thirst for righteousness, for they shall be filled.* MATTHEW5:6. Only God can get justice for His righteousness; we are not kingdom vigilantes. *...he hath done marvelous things: his right hand, and his holy arm, hath gotten him the victory. The LORD hath made known his salvation: his righteousness hath he openly shewed in the sight of the heathen. He hath remembered his mercy and his truth toward the house of Israel: all the ends of the earth have seen the salvation of our God.* PSALMS 98:1-3.

- *You have heard that it was said, you shall love your neighbor and hate your enemy.*
  - *...But I say to you, love your enemies, bless those who curse you, do good to those who hate you, and pray for those who spitefully use you and persecute you, that you may be sons of your Father in heaven; for He makes His sun rise on the evil and on the good, and sends rain on the just and on the unjust. For if you love those who love you, what reward have you? Do not even the tax collectors do the same? And if you*

*greet your brethren only, what do you do more than others? Do not even the tax collectors do so? Therefore, you shall be perfect, just as your Father in heaven is perfect.* MATTHEW 5:43-48.

Mature and perfect love always performs that which is not normal or expected. Your enemies want you to be selfish and narcissistic. Narcissism is the playground of the enemy and they are good at that game. Imagine how off putting your perfect and mature love will make your enemy feel. The enemy will never understand how you can Love without falling into powerless, hateful, feckless despair. Be the man God created in his image and put away childish things. *Thou shalt love thy neighbor as thyself...* MATTHEW 22:35-40.

- *And when you pray, you shall not be like the hypocrites. For they love to pray standing in the synagogues and on the corners of the streets, that they may be seen by men.*
  - *Assuredly I say to you, they have their reward. But you, when you pray, go into your room, and when you have shut your door, pray to your Father who is in the secret place; ...And when you pray, do not use vain repetitions as the heathen do. ...Therefore, do not be like them. For your Father knows the things you have need of before you ask Him.* MATTHEW 6:5-9.

*...in the morning, rising up a great while before day, He went out, and departed into a solitary place, and there He prayed.* MARK1:35. Praying is most probably the one activity that Jesus did more than any other. When you pray you invite Kingdom Influence into your physical space to change spirits, conditions, minds, and culture. Praying is a private activity that doesn't require the stamp of approval from spectators. We should never use public display of prayer and worship to impress men with our piety. We should never use prayer to puff up ourselves with our own self-importance. *Ye shall know them by their fruits... every good tree bringeth forth good fruit; ...Wherefore by their fruits ye shall know them.* MATTHEW 7:16-20. My tree shall yield fruit even in the land of my

affliction and even in drought. Men will be able to identify me by the fruit I bare.

*The LORD is gracious, and full of compassion; ... The LORD is good to all: and his tender mercies are over all his works. All thy works shall praise thee, O LORD; and thy saints shall bless thee. They shall speak of the glory of thy kingdom, and talk of thy power; To make known to the sons of men his mighty acts, and the glorious majesty of his kingdom. Thy kingdom is an everlasting kingdom, and thy dominion endureth throughout all generations. The LORD upholdeth all that fall, and raiseth up all those that be bowed down. The eyes of all wait upon thee; and thou givest them their meat in due season. Thou openest thine. hand, and satisfiest the desire of every living thing. The LORD is righteous in all his ways, and holy in all his works. The LORD is nigh unto all them that call upon him, to all that call upon him in truth. He will fulfil the desire of them that fear him: he also will hear their cry, and will save them. The LORD preserveth all them that love him: but all the wicked he will destroy.* PSALMS 145:8-20.

# Kingdom: Not Religion

GOD Says "Bring Me Out of the Abstract"

GENESIS 1:26-28

G od said, "*Let Us make man in Our image, according to Our likeness; let them have dominion over the fish of the sea, over the birds of the air, and over the cattle, over all the earth and over every creeping thing that creeps on the earth*". ...*Then God blessed them, and God said to them, "Be fruitful and multiply; fill the earth and subdue it; have dominion over the fish of the sea, over the birds of the air, and over every living thing that moves on the earth*". GENESIS 1:26-28. *The Lord God planted a garden eastward in Eden, and there He put the man whom He had formed* GENESIS 2:8.

*Lift your eyes now and look from the place where you are northward, southward, eastward, and westward; for all the land which you see I give to you and your descendants forever.* GENESIS 13:14-15. *In the same day the LORD made a covenant with Abram, saying, unto thy seed have I given this land, from the river of Egypt unto the great river, the river Euphrates: The Kenites, the Kenizzites, the Kadmonites, the Hittites, the Perizzites, the Rephaims, the Amorites, the Canaanites, the Girgashites, and the Jebusites.* GENESIS 15:19-21

Why Kingdom and not religion? God said let man have dominion over all the earth. God showed Abram the territory where He would put the new nation. A territory filled with men living by their own set of precepts, concepts and philosophies. However, Abraham was restricted by God from adopting the cultures in the territory with the expressed purpose to bring the territory under the influence of the Kingdom of Heaven. Displacing the foreign ideas, with the sovereign dominion idea of God. God gave Abraham and the nation His own ideas, culture, values, ethics, and disciplines.; *the kingdom of heaven has arrived. ...You shall not bow down to their gods, nor serve them, nor do according to their works;* EXODUS 23:24-33.

Man was created in the image and the likeness, of the invisible God, and fortified with His Spirit *...breathed into his nostrils the breath of life; and man became a living soul.* GENESIS 2:7. After the man became a living soul, he was placed in the presence of the invisible God. The visible man was mandated to have dominion, to rule, to be fruitful and to fill the earth. The visible Adam was created to mirror the nature and character of the invisible God and the invisible Kingdom of Heaven in an organized and governed visible domain. The citizens of the earth should pursue to walk like the King, talk like the King and live just like the King. Citizens of the earth are fully expected to follow the laws and righteousness of the invisible God. *...the Lord God commanded the man, saying, of every tree of the garden thou may freely eat:* GENESIS 2:16. The man was then given access to all things on the earth. Along with great power and unfettered access the visible man was also given a boundary; *but of the fruit of the tree which is in the midst of the garden, God hath said, Ye shall not eat of it, neither shall ye touch it, lest ye die.* GENESIS 3:2-3. The man had access to everything but he didn't own anything. Adam was the only created spirit fortified being who had accountability. Adam had to be fruitful, he had to dress and keep the place that God prepared, he was charged to fill the earth.

God spoke to create; Adam spoke to creation. *...the Lord God formed every beast of the field, and every fowl of the air; and brought them unto Adam to see what he would call them: and whatsoever Adam called every living creature that was the name thereof.* GENESIS 2:19.

The fellowship between the invisible and the visible was so proficient and efficient that Adam could hear the voice of God walking, *...they heard the voice of the LORD God walking in the garden in the cool of the day...*

GENESIS 3:8. As the invisible God created the earth, He struck a covenant with the visible man. Through this covenant the unseen invisible creator had fellowship with the seen visible created man. God abides in **the spirit realm**, beyond the perception of our visual or audible senses. However, Adam did have what we might identify as situational awareness, the environmental perception of the divine presence of the Great I Am. God is not limited by the physical laws and dimensions that govern creation. Nevertheless, Adam was able to hear **the voice of the LORD God walking....** The most important concept to understand is that nowhere in Genesis did the invisible God ever establish or institute any religion. The Kingdom of God is the influence of the Kingdom of Heaven on the earth, it is not a religion.

God prepared a place for Adam and put him in His presence. *...in the day that the Lord God made the earth and the heavens before any plant of the field was in the earth and before any herb of the field had grown. For the Lord God had not caused it to rain on the earth, and there was no man to till the ground;* GENESIS 2:4-5. The previous quoted text reveals the significance of the man and the man's assigned placement. There was no increase in the earth until Adam was created to till the ground. The most-sincere act of worship is for the son to aspire to be like his Father. In the New Testament Jesus is recorded to say "my father is always working." *"...My Father has been working until now, and I have been working."* JOHN 5:17. God created the man and the man was given work.

*Again, the kingdom of heaven is like unto a merchant man, seeking goodly pearls: who, when he had found one pearl of great price, went and sold all that he had, and bought it.* MATTHEW 13:45. The Kingdom of God is the pearl by which all human inspired governments will be measured. Jesus never taught religion. Jesus spent three years teaching his disciples about the virtues of the Kingdom of Heaven and demonstrating how the government of His kingdom works. Jesus came to redeem man and to re-establish His Kingdom. To say that Jesus established a religion is to categorize the Son of God, putting him on the same level as all other religious ideologues. Abraham was restricted by God from adopting the cultures in the territory with the expressed purpose to bring the territory under the influence of the Kingdom of Heaven.

John the Baptist came preaching in the wilderness of Judea. John would prepare the way of the Lord. *In those days came John the Baptist, preaching in the wilderness of Judaea, and saying, Repent ye: for the kingdom of heaven is at hand.* MATTHEW 3:1-2. Jesus was baptized by John, to identify with the Kingdom school of thought. A shared outlook of philosophy, discipline, belief, and cultural identification. Jesus, the Son of God, identified with John and not with the Pharisees.... *the kingdom of heaven is at hand.* Jesus, a master teacher of his time often used colloquialisms from the Kingdom school of psychology, words such as the word repent, *"Repent, for the kingdom of heaven is at hand."* MATTHEW4:17.

*...And he said unto them, I must preach the kingdom of God to other cities also: for therefore am I sent.* LUKE 4:43. Jesus came to earth to retrieve His system and re-establish His Kingdom on the earth. Jesus began preaching and teaching in a territory under Greek influence, and Roman occupation. From this point and for the next three years we can identify the priority of Jesus, to preach the Kingdom of God. Remember Jesus never preached democracy or religion. Jesus came to establish his ekklesia to manage and administer the will of the King on the earth.

Jesus began his ministry teaching; *"Repent, for the kingdom of heaven is at hand"* MATTHEW4:17. The word repent is not a call to remorse. The word repent is from the school of psychology, *from the Greek metanoia- (after thought, to change one's mind or purpose, indicating change or to have mental perception, mind and thought; a transformative change of heart).* In the King James Version of the Bible, its verbal cognate is translated as repent. Men are challenged by Jesus to a personal, absolute surrender to God as Sovereign. Though it includes sorrow and regret, it is significantly more. In other words, change your way of thinking to change your way of living. **"*Repent, for the kingdom of heaven is at hand"*** is the Jesus way of telling us that we are following the wrong bread crumbs, headed in the wrong direction. Jesus never preached or taught any religion. We need to stop following bad ideas, bad concepts, and bad principles. We need to change our priorities to **seek the kingdom of God, and his righteousness first.** Change our way of thinking to change our way of living. *Therefore, if any man be in Christ, he is a new creature: old things are passed away; behold, all things are become new.* 2 CORINTHIANS 5:17. We need to repent.

Jesus once said that the kingdom is like a treasure. *...the kingdom of heaven is like treasure hidden in a field, which a man found and hid; and for joy over it he goes and sells all that he has and buys that field.* MATTHEW 13:44. When men discover the treasure of the Kingdom of God, they will give up all they know to gain access to the Kingdom. Man was created to live with a legitimate efficient government of great integrity where wealth, justice, and peace are common. The fifth chapter of New Testament Matthew goes further to voice the antithesis of Jesus. Straight from the voice of the King, the Son of God, we hear and learn what the religious have never understood about Jesus or the laws of His Kingdom.

The lexicon or vernacular of the bible is that of a King and a kingdom. The Genesis story uses words such as *dominion over, subdue it, let them rule;* these words do not imply religion; however, they do convey government. The Kingdom of God will establish righteousness, boundaries, and order. Religion is too abstract and subject to the perception of men to sustain order. In the absence of government men are left to anarchy *...there was no king in Israel, but every man did that which was right in his own eyes.* JUDGES 17:6. Jesus preached *...as ye go, preach, saying, the kingdom of heaven is at hand.* MATTHEW 10:7.

The territory is the sovereign personal property belonging to the King. The words "*The Lord*" appear over 2400 times in the bible text, demonstrating ownership. *The earth is the Lord's, and the fullness thereof; the world, and they that dwell therein.* PSALMS 24:1. This is why we affirm "*Jesus is Lord!*". God used Abraham to birth a nation. Jesus died to redeem the nation. The Apostles came to disciple the nations. *Paul dwelt two whole years in his own hired house, and received all that came in unto him, and without hindrance he preached the kingdom of God and taught about the Lord Jesus Christ.* ACTS 28:30-31. Religion was never the priority of these men.

Adam, through one single act of disobedience, drove man from the fellowship with the invisible God. We will now have to be content that God will be with us, keeping the relationship alive. Jesus came to the hood. Jesus with one single act of obedience came to earth to be numbered among the transgressors. The Lord walks with man through the valley and the shadow of death. Just before Jesus gave up the ghost and died, He turned to one of the men with whom He was hanging. In a response to the one single moment of faith Jesus declared that the dying man can now be with him in paradise. *Verily I say unto thee, today shalt thou be with me in paradise.* LUKE 23:43.

*I am crucified with Christ: nevertheless, I live; yet not I, but Christ liveth in me: and the life which I now live in the flesh I live by the faith of the Son of God, who loved me, and gave himself for me.* GALATIANS 2:20. We should echo the words of Apostle Paul. The old life filled with corruption, deception, and disobedience was crucified. The old life of narcissism and selfishness has been crucified. The priority to gratify lust was crucified. I now live with Christ in restored fellowship, dominion, and inheritance. *Come, you blessed of My Father, inherit the kingdom prepared for you from the foundation of the world:* MATTHEW 25:34. The inheritance that is a Kingdom and not a religion. I will not leave my neighbor victimized and bleeding on the side of the road in the life that I now live. I will not devalue my brother in the life that I now live. I will gather fragments in the life that I now live. I can be fruitful by the faith of the Son of God in this land of my affliction. I will manifest and mirror the nature, character, virtues and righteousness of the invisible God. God will be with me and I can be with the invisible God in the life that I now live.

Finally, and very briefly we turn our attention to the prophet Daniel who shares a vision given to him by the Ancient of days. Daniel describes an event where a Kingdom of, glory and dominion where all people, nations and languages will serve the King of the everlasting dominion which will never be destroyed. *And the kingdom and dominion, and the greatness of the kingdom under the whole heaven, shall be given to the people of the saints of the most High, whose kingdom is an everlasting kingdom, and all dominions shall serve and obey him.* DANIEL 7:13-27.

# Kingdom Temple

### The Temple that God Built

📖 GENESIS 2:7

All heads of state live in an official residence. The President lives in the White House. The Queen of England lives in Buckingham Palace. The Emperor of Japan lives in The Tokyo Imperial Palace. The King of Thailand lives in Royal residences of the Chakri Dynasty. The Pope lives in the Papal Palace at Vatican City. The Governor lives in the Governor's Mansion. Pilate lived in the Palace Compound built by Herod the Great. These residences also serve as the official address of official government business. The head of state will have to govern as he resides on the territory. The President of the United States cannot govern the US and live in Canada.

God created man in his image and likeness, fortified him with His Spirit. God, gave man dominion over the earth mandating the man to fill the earth, to rule and be fruitful. God *...breathed into his nostrils the breath of life; and man became a living soul.* GENESIS 2:7. The man who became a living soul became a living temple. *... The Lord God planted a garden eastward in Eden, and there He put the man whom He had formed* GENESIS 2:8. God created a place where He planted the living temple. God will abide in the living temple, the official residence of the domain under the dominion of the Holy King. The living temple is the official residence of the Holy, Sovereign King. It is where the holy fellowship of the invisible God and the physical visible man was established. *The words that I speak to you I do not speak on my own authority; but the Father who dwells* *in me...I am in the Father and the Father in Me...*JOHN 14:7-11. That quote is the testimony of the holy fellowship.

The sanctuary is for the man. The sanctuary is where we can find immunity from the stress of life. I will dwell in the secret place of the Most-High. I shall abide under the shadow of the Almighty. The high tower is where I can find refuge, security, and protection from terrors and violent arrows launched by my enemies. The sanctuary is my fortress protecting me from destruction and perilous pestilence. The sanctuary is a hiding place for me. *"He is my refuge and my fortress; My God, in Him I will trust."* ...*He shall cover you with His feathers, and under His wings you shall take refuge;* PSALMS 91:1-6; PSALMS 144:2. PSALMS 61:3; PSALMS 119:114; PSALMS 3:3; 2 SAMUEL 22:3. *The Lord God planted a garden eastward in Eden, and there He put the man whom He had formed* GENESIS 2:8. The green pastures is where He makes me lie down. *He maketh me to lie down in green pastures:* PSALMS 23. *Thou wilt keep him in perfect peace, whose mind is stayed on thee: because he trusteth in thee.* ISAIAH 26:3; The garden He put is where He planted me in the sanctuary.

The Holy Temple is expressly, for the Holy King. The King of Glory shall be in his Holy Temple. The Temple will display His Glory, His excellence, and His majesty. His influence is without restriction in His Holy Temple. The Temple is the Holy place where the Holy God abides. The King will assert his sovereign creative ownership rights to build the Temple to His pleasure; *...as it seemed good to the potter to make* JEREMIAH 18:1-11. The Holy *Lord will sit upon his throne, high and lifted up, and his train will fill the Temple.* ISAIAH 6:1. There will be no room for anything unholy or unrighteous. The Temple where no-thing is secret and all things are revealed. Man cannot hide behind fig leaves in the Holy Temple. Every single thought will be available to The Holy King. Every emotion will be exposed to the Holy King. The King will see the depths of my heart and love me the same. I may be able to hide contemplations from man but I can't hide them from the Holy King in the Holy Temple. The Temple is for the Holy One.

God abides in *the spirit realm*, beyond the perception of our visual or audible senses. However, in the Temple the unseen invisible creator has fellowship with the seen visible created man. The fellowship was so secure that Adam was able to hear *the voice of the LORD God walking....* When Adam abdicated authority and forfeited it to the prince of darkness, leaving the world to an illegal, illegitimate, counterfeit control, he was driven from the presence of God. As time passed the wickedness of man became great in the earth, and every intent of his heart made man lose sight of the priority of God, *dominion over the earth. ...My spirit shall not always strive with man...* GENESIS 6:3. Man lost the fellowship of the Temple and now he has to wait for God to be with him. He can no longer be with his King. There is no fellowship between righteousness and unrighteousness. There is no communion between light and darkness.

I have been blessed enough to visit Sacré Coeur and Notre Dame de Paris. I have been to Westminster Abbey and St Paul's Cathedral in London. Some friends talked me into a helicopter tour of Kilauea, in Hawaii. I have been privileged to see the Grand Canyon, Hoover Dam, and Niagara Falls. I have been from Maine to Florida, from Mobile to New Orleans to Lake Charles. I have driven across Glacier National Park. Once I drove on the Pacific Coast Highway from Los Angeles to the San Francisco Bay Area. I have been blessed to visit London, Ireland, Paris, Aruba, Guam, and The Bahamas. I have driven across the prairies of Texas, the deserts of Arizona and the Rocky Mountains of Montana. Not one of these places will compare to the one single *solitary place* where I can be with my Holy God and King in the Holy Temple. I can be the real me, with no pretentions, no smokescreens, no false impressions. The place where I live, move and have my being. ACTS 17:28. There is no fellowship like the fellowship in the Temple with the Holy God.

*Eye hath not seen, nor ear heard, neither have entered into the heart of man, the things which God hath prepared for them that love him. But God hath revealed them unto us by his Spirit: ...*

*Now we have received, not the spirit of the world, but the spirit which is of God; that we might know the things that are freely given to us of God...*1 CORINTHIANS 2:9-15. Paul quotes Isaiah in the Corinthian text. However, Isaiah didn't know the abiding of the Holy Spirit. Paul on the other hand makes this statement after the blood of Christ has cleaned the Temple that was defiled by disobedience. The cleaned Temple is once again free to the Holy King and the King has returned to the Holy Temple. The fellowship in the Holy Temple is like no other fellowship. I can hear the voice of my Holy King as he speaks to me. In this Holy place the Holy King is with me and I can be with the Holy King. The King has redeemed me and cleaned his Temple. I can now live by the faith of the Son of God.

I am His Temple. I can share all of my heart with the Holy King. I will never be able to hide anything from the invisible God. The Holy God will see me in all my nakedness and He will know me. After knowing all the things I may attempt to hide the Holy King will not cast me away. I will draw neigh to Him and He will draw nigh to me. The Holy King will make known all things unto me and guide me to all truth. I will adore, esteem, and worship the King in His Temple.

When we, the citizens elect a new governor the old governor will have to move out and the newly elected governor will move into the mansion. When Jesus, the Son of God, died as a man we were redeemed. *the father said to his servants, bring forth the best robe, and put it on him; and put a ring on his hand, and shoes on his feet.* LUKE 15:22. The father restored our legitimate identity, our inheritance, and our peace. We have been *returned, recovered, recycled, reconciled, renewed, restored,* we have been *redeemed.* The Son of God gave his blood to sweep and clean the house. Now the legitimate governor, The Holy Spirit can move back into the governor's mansion. *...know ye not that your body is the temple of the Holy Ghost which is in you, which ye have of God,* ...1 CORINTHIANS 6:19.

# Kingdom Efficiency

### The Way God Does Things!

📖MATTHEW14:15-21

Kingdom efficiency is about the way God does things.

When this idea came to me, my first thought was how to explain kingdom efficiency to religious people. The word efficient is not a religious word and it doesn't appear in the bible text. I waited for the Holy Spirit to advise me. Early one morning I heard the Spirit of God say… *"it is about the way God does things"* …. *"how things get done in the Kingdom"*. I grew up hearing that the Lord moves in mysterious ways. However, as I grew up in the Lord, I learned that God's ways are not as mysterious as they are different. *"**For my thoughts are not your thoughts, neither are your ways my ways**"* …. ISAIAH 55:8. Jesus was often time heard saying; ***The kingdom of heaven is like…*** The Kingdom of God is different. We should never expect God to do or say the predictable things that we hear ordinary men do or say. So, I started in Genesis scouring the scriptures to find stories that clearly show that the Kingdom of Heaven is indeed efficient. I barely scratched the surface.

The earth was without form, it was void, and it was dark. The Holy Spirit arrived bringing order and structure. In the Genesis story God said let there be light and the sun became the center of the solar system bringing light, warmth, and energy. God spoke and the atmosphere was divided into five main layers. The troposphere, the stratosphere, the mesosphere, the thermosphere and the exosphere. God said that the earth should bring forth grasses and trees. The grasses and trees should bring forth herbs and fruit. The fruit should bring forth seed that produces after its own kind. This cycle qualifies sowing and reaping as a perpetual event of creation. The skies and seas were filled with birds and fish that produce after their kind. The cattle and four-legged beast were filled with seed to produce after their own kind.

Then God prepared a place for the man and there, God put the man. *The Lord God planted a garden eastward in Eden, and there He put the man*...-GENESIS 2:8. *And the Lord said unto Abram, ... Lift up now thine eyes, and look from the place where thou art northward, and southward, and eastward, and westward: For all the land which thou seest, to thee will I give it, and to thy seed forever. ...I will give it unto thee.* GENESIS 13:14-17. *He maketh me to lie down in green pastures: PSALMS* 23. *Arise, go to Zarephath, ...and dwell there.* -1 KINGS 17:9. God will always prepare us for a place that He has prepared for us. We can now influence the territory with the ideas of the Sovereign Creator, having been created in His image and likeness and fortified with His Spirit. We are well able to manifest His values, culture, and His will in the territory. Man, who is fortified with the Spirit of God asserts the influence of the Kingdom of Heaven through the Kingdom of God... *Thy kingdom come. Thy will be done in earth, as it is in heaven...* MATTHEW 6:10

*God blessed them,* GENESIS 1:26-28. God would hardly give dominion of the earth to an unstable, unbalanced, unhappy man so he blessed them. God fortified the man with a good disposition and a sense of wellbeing, he wanted the man to be happy. If the man is unhappy and frustrated, he will not be able to accomplish the God given mandate. A dysfunctional man will be inefficient putting creation at risk. *Male and female created he them; and blessed them, and called their name Adam, in the day when they were created.* GENESIS 5:2.

The average human adult male is approximately 60% water. Water carries oxygen and nutrients to cells in the body through the blood. Water helps to cushion our joints. Water is also used to help digest and absorb food. Without water a man could die in as little as three days. Water is used to flush waste out of our bodies. So, is it any wonder that of all the mineral resources in the earth water is so easily accessible? Seventy-one percent of the earth's surface is covered by water. The place where God put the man had four rivers and water could be readily found on the surface. There are oceans, seas, and rivers to provide transportation routes for industrial freight. Lakes provides access in valleys, plateaus, and places far from the coastal areas. Glaciers help to cover the mountains. Gold has to be mined, Onyx and other precious stone have to be excavated. Oil has to be drilled. God made sure that man's access to water would be without restriction. God's creation is efficient.

Adam had work while living in the garden, *...the Lord God formed every beast of the field, and every fowl of the air; and brought them unto Adam to see what he would call them: and whatsoever Adam called every living creature that was the name thereof.* -GENESIS 2:19. This is the testimony that Adam was well able to complete any work that God assigned him to accomplish. A great example of maximum productivity with minimum effort. God's idea for Adam was work. The idea of toil and sweat, which is inefficient, came after Adam decided to rebel against God. *...In toil you shall eat of it all the days of your life. Both thorns and thistles it shall bring forth for you, and you shall eat the herb of the field. In the sweat of your face, you shall eat bread...*GENESIS 3:17. Man's disobedience reduced him to manual inefficient living.

The children of Israel did not end up in Egypt by accident. They are there by God's efficient design. Joseph declared to his brothers "*...God sent me before you to preserve life.*" -GENESIS 45:5,7. God did what I call divine in vitro fertilization. God took the seed of one nation and placed that seed in the womb of another nation, and after a four-hundred-year gestation period a new nation was born. Being intimidated by the presence of the children of Israel the Pharaoh of Egypt was motivated to force the people into servitude. The Pharaoh's reputation was at risk and he needed to prove that he was in control. Pharaoh forced the people of Israel to sweat and toil for his glory. The Pharaoh made the mistake thinking he could exploit the people of another king. The Pharaoh's behavior foolishly opened a door and the God that he thought so little of demonstrated that He is indeed Lord. However, God did not move against Pharaoh with raw naked aggression. God moved in a much more efficient manner.

The Pharaoh of Egypt came face to face with the God who could answer the question, who and what army. ... *Thus, says the Lord: By this you shall know that I am the Lord. ...I will strike the waters which are in the river with the rod that is in my hand, and they shall be turned to blood.* EXODUS 7:17. The Pharaoh was about to experience the greatest most powerful efficient demonstration of biological warfare ever witnessed. During the attack on Aleppo the water supply was controlled by different warring factions in a way to put pressure on the opposite side. Attack all the utilities, water, power, gas, and communications and you can take the territory. When God struck the water, the water became a weapon. The offensive strike against the territory infrastructure leaves the enemy exposed. The warfare will then become more intense. *Behold ...I will smite all your territory with frogs. So, the river shall bring forth frogs abundantly, which shall go up and come into your house, into your bedroom, on your bed, into the houses of your servants, on your people, into your ovens, and into your kneading bowls. I will send swarms of flies on you and your servants, on your people and into your houses.* EXODUS 8:2-3. The people were overwhelmed with salmonella infected frogs. Salmonella can spread by either direct or indirect contact with amphibians like frogs, and other reptiles or their droppings. Pharaoh's people didn't have clean water to clean up after the frogs that were everywhere and there were no sanitizing wipes. Don't forget about the flies. The germy little creatures began to spread dangerous bacteria from manure and rotting food. Then to add insult to injury *...I will bring locusts into your territory. And they shall cover the face of the earth, so that no one will be able to see the earth; ...and they shall eat every tree, which grows up for you out of the field.* EXODUS 10:4-5. Agriculture was a major part of Egypt's economy. The attack on the economic structure is another way to bring down a territory. Attacking food supplies is an efficient way to bring suffering to enemy territory maximizing pressure. This is what contemporary governments refer to as sanctions.

Later that same day, a nation of people, men, women, and children were under the pursuit of an army of thundering warriors, chariots, and horses. The Pharaoh thought that he had the upper hand and the people were cornered by the sea. There was nowhere to run. Just as it seemed it was all over. *...the Lord overthrew the Egyptians in the midst of the sea. Then the waters returned and covered the chariots, the horsemen, and all the army of Pharaoh that came into the sea after them.* God's offensive attack was so efficient that Egypt's entire army was destroyed. ***Not so much as one of them remained.*** EXODUS 14:27–28.

*So it was, whenever Israel had sown, Midianites would come up; also, Amalekites and the people of the East would come up against them. Then they would encamp against them and destroy the produce of the...and leave no sustenance for Israel...coming in as numerous as locusts; both they and their camels were without number; and they would enter the land to destroy it.* JUDGES 6:3-6. Gideon's response was typical. Gideon's approach was to match the aggression he saw with his own. So, he gathered as many men as he could to answer the hostility of the enemy. The problem with Gideon's approach was that his approach was not efficient. God then sent Gideon a tweet telling him "***The people who are with you are too many...***" JUDGES 7:2. If Gideon was going to save Israel from the hand of the Midianites and give God glory for doing it, he was going to have to do this God's way. So, at God's command the thirty-two thousand men that Gideon thought he needed were cut down to three hundred. *"O my Lord, how can I save Israel? ...my clan is the weakest in Manasseh, and I am the least in my father's house."* JUDGES 6:15. The insecure Gideon was expected to defeat a crushing enemy with only three hundred men. Yes! God was so efficient that Gideon needed only the three hundred men that God left with him. God with Gideon and three hundred men were so efficient that the enemy retreated. When the three hundred men blew their trumpets, *the Lord set every man's sword against his companion throughout the whole camp; and the army fled...* JUDGES 7:22.

Jonathan, the son of King Saul, and a young man that bare his armor came face to face with a garrison of the Philistines. Jonathan was not afraid to face the garrison, *"…The Lord will work for us: for there is no restraint to the Lord to save by many or by few."* 1ST SAMUEL 14:6 Jonathan and his armor bearer made themselves known to the garrison and when the Philistines called out to them the fight was on. After the fight was over Jonathan and the armor bearer looked over a half-acre of land filled with dead bodies.

Many of us grew up hearing the story of David and Goliath. David, the youngest of the eight sons of Jesse, was a shepherd who was proficient feeding and protecting sheep. Goliath was described as a Philistine giant, a man of combat who knew how to wage warfare. Goliath was known for bullying, threating, and taunting Israel. As the story goes David and Goliath come face to face in a mix-matched clash encounter. It appeared that David was outmatched. Goliath's aggression must have seemed overpowering. Sometimes a man can find himself in situations that seem insurmountable. In his human wisdom, the King thought to give his amour to David. An old testament version of a bad man with a gun versus a good man with a gun. *…David said unto Saul, I cannot go with these; for I have not proved them. And David put them off him. …he took his staff in his hand, and chose him five smooth stones out of the brook, and put them in a shepherd's bag which he had, even in a scrip; and his sling was in his hand: and he drew near to the Philistine.* 1 SAMUEL 17:39-40. David knew that if God delivered him from a lion and a bear surely God could deliver him from the Philistine. David knew it would be inefficient to use a weapon he was never train with or a weapon he never used. We often have ideas that appear to be a solution and the answer to our dilemma only to find out our thoughts and our ways are inefficient. Therefore, a good man with a gun is not the answer. David had backup known as the Lord of Host and he knew that the Lord would not let him go down in defeat. *…David to the Philistine, Thou comest to me with a sword, and with a spear, and with a shield: but I come to thee in the name of the LORD of hosts, the God of the armies of Israel, whom thou hast defied.* 1 SAMUEL 17:45

Jesus shares another parable about the way God does things, specifically how things get done in the Kingdom. *...The kingdom of heaven is likened unto a man which sowed good seed in his field: But while men slept, his enemy came and sowed tares among the wheat, and went his way.* MATTHEW 13:24-25. Isn't it just like the enemy to create a big mess and leave you hanging? However, the enemy did not count on an informed landowner who knew the field, the sowers, and the reapers; *...when the blade was sprung up, and brought forth fruit, then appeared the tares also.* MATTHEW 13:26. The sowers thought they had a solution. However, the landowner understood that the sowers solution was more of a reaction. The landowner knew that the sowers proposal would put the harvest at risk. *...The servants said unto him, wilt thou then that we go and gather them up?* MATTHEW 13:28 The landowner also knew that sowers were not reapers. The landowner knew the difference in the expertise and specialties. *But he said, Nay; lest while ye gather up the tares, ye root up also the wheat with them. Let both grow together until the harvest: and in the time of harvest, I will say to the reapers, gather ye together first the tares, and bind them in bundles to burn them: but gather the wheat into my barn.* MATTHEW 13:24-30. The reapers knew the when, the where, and the how of reaping. The plot of the enemy failed and the enemy did not prosper.

As a multitude followed him, Jesus had been preaching and healing the sick in the desert. The disciples noticed the late hour and they alerted Jesus that the people needed to eat. The best idea the disciples could come up with was to send them away so they could get food. Jesus response to them was.... *"They need not depart; give ye them to eat."* MATTHEW 14:16. There was no convention center staff on duty and no conference committee to work out the logistics of feeding so many people in the desert. The only food available to them was five loaves and two fishes. Jesus said... *"Bring them to me."* After the people sat down Jesus took the loaves and gave thanks, distributed the bread to the disciples and began to feed the people. There was no chaos, no shoving, and no pushing. There was order and obedience and the people were fed. When they were finished, Jesus ordered the disciples to gather up all that was left so that none would be lost, a great example of Kingdom efficiency. Jesus wrote the book on recycling. There was more than enough to feed all the men, women, and children. When it was all over there was more left over than when they began. I am sure there are many CEOs wishing they could do that. Jesus insisted that not one crumb be thrown away. What a great lesson in Kingdom Efficiency. The Kingdom can take what the world would consider insufficient and achieve maximum productivity with minimum waste. MATTHEW 14

As Jesus prepared to feed the multitude, he stopped long enough to give thanks for what was so obviously not enough. By today's fiscal standards it would seem redundant to show thankfulness when we know we are so short changed. Our resources are seemingly insufficient. How are we going to make the resources stretch? How are we going to make it through with less than enough? How are we going to make ends meet? Kingdom culture teaches us to give thanks even where there is not enough. Our thankfulness will manifest more than enough. Thankfulness added to faith will make life more efficient.

*I shall not want* testifies that the Kingdom of God is efficient. Things in the Kingdom are done well. *...He hath done all things well: he makes both the deaf to hear, and the dumb to speak.* MARK 7:37. No citizen wants to live under a wasteful dysfunctional king.

Kingdom culture teaches us to give thanks for not enough. Our thankfulness will manifest sufficiency. As a matter of fact, thankfulness added to faith equals more than enough.

# Kingdom Identity

## Do You Know Who You Are?

☐MATTHEW16:13-16

**I** **AM** *that* I AM: ... *thou say unto the children of Israel,* I AM *hath sent me unto you.* EXODUS 3:13-14. The sovereign creator who truly "**exist**" has identified himself as **I AM.** Know that the sun shines without any interruption because **I AM** spoke the words *"let there be light".* Tectonic plates have been shifting ever since **I AM** spoke the words *"let the dry land appear",* creating ocean trenches, volcanic mountains, and islands. After the hurricanes bring storm surges the water recedes because **I AM** spoke and the waters gathered together in one place. **I AM** spoke separating the salt waters from the fresh waters. When **I AM** spoke to the surface waters, they begin to separate creating the troposphere, stratosphere, mesosphere, thermosphere, and the exosphere. It is the integrity of **I AM** that guarantees the trees will bud in February, the winds will blow in March, the showers will fall in April, and the flowers will bloom in May.

*Then God said, Let Us make man in Our image, according to Our likeness; let them have dominion over the fish of the sea, over the birds of the air, and over the cattle, over all the earth and over every creeping thing that creeps on the earth... Then God blessed them, and God said to them, be fruitful and multiply; fill the earth and subdue it; have dominion over the fish of the sea, over the birds of the air, and over every living thing that moves on the earth. So, God created man in his own image, in the image of God created he him; male and female created he them* GENESIS 1:26-28.

Adam was the first victim of identity theft. Lucifer having no integrity, no reputation, and no-good name stole authentic identity to gain control of the world systems. Not only did the thief want to steal Adam's identity, he wanted to assume it as well. Being the thief and liar that he is, Lucifer had no problem using someone else's reputation to achieve his diabolical agenda. Lucifer, who was created for heaven and not for earth, cannot assert any rights to the control of the territory because he is illegitimate. He tells the first lie, committing the very first act of identity theft. Lucifer, driven by pride and lust conspired to commit rebellion that was crushed in a flash; *...I beheld Satan as lightning fall from heaven.* LUKE 10:18. The dissenting angel who was created for heaven, was motivated to control the territory and the only way he could ever get that control was to take what he knew was not lawfully his. Lucifer needed a legitimate identity to establish his illegitimate regime, asserting illegal and counterfeit control of the world systems.

Man was created in the image and likeness of God. Man identifies with God the Father through divine DNA. The loss of true identity can damage reputation, credibility and integrity. This loss impedes affluence and weakens influence. The theft of identity destroys privilege and advantages that go with a good name. This case of identity theft plunged man into the worst case of identity crisis ever. As long as there is an identity crisis there will be crisis of destiny and until man gets his identity back life will be a struggle. Lucifer wants to impose a false image and identity. The abuse we suffer, no matter if it is physical or psychological comes to re-define us. *...O house of Israel, cannot I do with you as this potter? ...Behold, as the clay is in the potter's hand, so are ye in mine hand,* JEREMIAH 18:1-11. God calls us kings, priests, sons, and ambassadors. If we start being who God called us to be, we can do what God created us to do. We need to stop the Clark Kent impersonation, get rid of the phone booth mentality, to walk in true destiny. We must be the Sons that God created us to be. We are not physical beings having a spiritual experience. Rather, we are spiritual beings having a temporal experience. The one who did not create us doesn't get to re-image us or steal our identity.

To walk in true destiny man must walk in true identity. Jacob whose name meant supplanter was given a new name. *... Thy name is Jacob: thy name shall not be called any more Jacob, but Israel shall be thy name: and he called his name Israel.* GENESIS 35:10. Just like that Jacob was no longer identified as a cheater but as a legitimate son. As we pursue Kingdom of God, we are not murderers, fornicators, liars, or thieves. Satan understands the true significance of legitimate identity and he wants to snatch our destiny. Until Moses discovered that he was not the son of Egypt but rather the son of slaves he was not able to manifest his true destiny.

The most powerful relationship in the Kingdom is the one between the father and the son. *... Let Us make man in Our image, according to Our likeness...* GENESIS 1:26-28. Words are ideas conceived and expressed, from precept to concept. Jesus is the word made flesh. Jesus is the *expressed* idea of God. *In the beginning was the Word, and the Word was with God, and the Word was God. The same was in the beginning with God. All things were made by him; and without him was not anything made that was made.* JOHN 1:1-3. Jesus was validated by his Father. Jesus is the Christ. Jesus is Lord, Jesus is King. Jesus is the Son of Man but Jesus is Son of God first. When Jesus, the Son of Man came to the hood he didn't identify with Rome or the Pharisees. Jesus Christ never identified with any traditional system of religion. Instead, Jesus identified with the forerunner John the Baptist who was preaching in the wilderness of Judea that the Kingdom of Heaven had arrived; *Repent ye: for the kingdom of heaven is at hand.* MATTHEW 3:1-2. Jesus was baptized by John, to identify with the master teacher and his school of thought.

Jesus is classically misunderstood. Jesus is more than just a wise man. Jesus is not one of 6 million gods. Jesus is not a highly-developed human with superior mental capacity. Jesus is not a failed prophet. Jesus is not the imagined creation of 12 misguided men. Jesus is not the founder of any religion. Jesus is not now nor ever was a pragmatist. We should never politicize Jesus; He isn't a conservative nor a liberal. Jesus should never be identified as politically correct. Jesus is not a superhero nor is Jesus prince charming. Superheroes risk their lives; Jesus gave his life. There are many misconceptions of Jesus Christ. Jesus is historically misunderstood. Even while He walked on the earth His greatest challenge came from religious people. They came asking who is this man and what is His message? While we may argue, debate, or doubt the true identity of Jesus, He knew exactly who he was. Jesus knew his purpose and his destiny. *...he steadfastly set his face to go to Jerusalem* LUKE 9:51 Jesus was so secure in His identity that he was *obedient unto death, even the death of the cross.* PHILIPPIANS 2:6-8. What is the point of calling Jesus King if we won't treat him like the King that He is? Jesus is King. Jesus is the Son of man. Jesus is the Son of God.

Meanwhile the devil, the self-imposed illegal authority, shows up to challenge Jesus while he was in the wilderness. *...If you are the Son of God, command this stone to become bread.* LUKE 4:3. Let's be clear, Satan was not confused about the identity of Jesus. More to the point. Jesus was not confused about His identity. However, Satan's narcissistic delusion gave him the boldness to step to the Lord and try to entice the Lord with property that the Lord already owns. The devil just couldn't seem to help himself. *And the devil said to Him, all this authority I will give You, and their glory; for this has been delivered to me, and I give it to whomever I wish. Therefore, if You will worship before me, all will be Yours.* LUKE 4:6-7. Satan's attempt to trip Jesus up was at best pointless. *All things were made by him; and without him was not anything made that was made.* JOHN 1:3. Let there be no mistake Jesus knew exactly who he was. Jesus understood his identity, his purpose, and his true destiny.

Jesus once asked his disciples; *... Whom do men say that I the Son of man am? Some said John, Elias, Jeremias or some other prophet. Then He asked them. "Whom say ye that I am?" Then Peter answered.... "Thou art the Christ, the Son of the living God'.* MATTHEW 16:13-18. The, legitimate, legal, anointed King has come to re-assert his authority in the earth and take back his property. He came to set up his government though his *ekklesia* to manage and administer the will of the King on the earth. *...a child is born and a son is given and the government shall be upon his shoulder; and his name shall be called Wonderful, Counselor, The mighty God, The everlasting Father, The Prince of Peace".* ISAIAH 9:6.

*If you had known me, you would have known My Father also; He who has seen me has seen the Father; ...Do you not believe that I am in the Father, and the Father in Me? The words that I speak to you I do not speak on my own authority; but the Father who dwells in me...I am in the Father and the Father in Me...*JOHN 14:7-11. The son sent by the Father is vested with legitimate sovereign authority....*when the fullness of the time was come, God sent forth his Son...*GALATIANS 4:4. The Son will be validated by the Father. *Thou art my beloved Son, in whom I am well pleased.* MARK 1:11. *... This is my beloved Son, in whom I am well pleased.* MATTHEW 3:17. Established legitimacy, rights, privileges, inheritance are imparted to the son. *Come, you blessed of My Father, inherit the kingdom prepared for you from the foundation of the world:* MATTHEW 25:34. *.... Wherefore, thou art no more a servant, but a son; and if a son, then an heir of God through Christ.* GALATIANS 4:7.

We are not a religious lobbing group, conservative or liberal. The ekklesia was never mandated to lobby for religious liberties. God put Adam in place to have dominion. Jesus the Christ established an ekklesia to redeem that dominion....*ye shall be unto me a kingdom of priests, and an holy nation.* EXODUS 19:6. *...ye are a chosen generation, a royal priesthood, a holy nation, a peculiar people;* 1 PETER 2:9. When the prodigal son returned to his father ...*the father said to his servants, bring forth the best robe, and put it on him; and put a ring on his hand, and shoes on his feet.* LUKE 15:22. The father restored the son's legitimate identity, he restored the son's inheritance and he restored the son's peace. The kingdom concept declares that identity as son is not gender specific. We are all sons, male and female created he them. The death of Christ restores man's legitimate identity through redemption. The legitimacy is rightfully ours because of the eternal inheritance. *But as many as received him, to them gave he power to become the sons of God,* JOHN 1:12.

*Beloved, now are we the sons of God...*1 JOHN 3:2. *For as many as are led by the Spirit of God, they are the sons of God....* ROMANS 8:14. *Henceforth I call you not servants; for the servant knoweth not what his lord doeth: but I have called you friends; for all things that I have heard of my Father I have made known unto you.* JOHN 15:15 *Now then we are ambassadors for Christ...*2 CORINTHIANS 5:20 Stop the Clark Kent impression and be the sons that God created us to be. *Come, you blessed of My Father, inherit the kingdom prepared for you from the foundation of the world:* MATTHEW 25:34.

# Kingdom Destiny

Appointment with Destiny

☐LUKE 4:43

We all know sometimes life hates and troubles can make you wish you were born in another time and space. But you can bet your lifetimes that and twice it's double. That God knew exactly where he wanted you to be placed.

*-Stevie Wonder*

Mankind was created with destiny and purpose. Many books have been written about purpose; however, this writing will focus on destiny. Destiny and Purpose are what I call twin companions. You cannot fulfill purpose without finding true destiny. Consider that destiny is the place where God wants you to be placed and purpose is what you do when you are in place.

While spending time studying scripture, I can identify at least five men who would provide great portraits of authentic destiny. As we begin this study let us remember Adam, Joseph, Moses, David, and Jesus.

Adam had the definitive destiny experience. Adam lived in the presence of God, fortified with the influence of God, with unfettered access of the creating God. He received the breath of the Spirit of God, becoming a living soul, and straightaway he walks in true destiny. The first man never had to compile an impressive resume, worry about his status in popularity poles, climb the corporate ladder, fight gridlock traffic, or build a lucrative annuity. He never had to overcome insecurity or low self-esteem. Adam wasn't mercenary or narcissistic. As God was able to speak to create, Adam was able to speak to creation. As I have said in the past having the definitive destiny Adam was living large. *...God said, "Let Us make man in Our image, according to Our likeness; let them have dominion over the fish of the sea, over the birds of the air, and over the cattle, over all*

*the earth and over every creeping thing that creeps on the earth". ...
"Be fruitful and multiply; fill the earth and subdue it; have dominion
over the fish of the sea, over the birds of the air, and over every living
thing that moves on the earth".* GENESIS 1:26-28 *...the Lord God formed
every beast of the field, and every fowl of the air; and brought them
unto Adam to see what he would call them: and whatsoever Adam
called every living creature that was the name thereof.* GENESIS 2:19

However, there was another being lurking about to disrupt the tranquility
of the earth. Lucifer having no integrity, no reputation, and no-good name
stole authentic identity to gain control of the world systems. Being the
thief and liar that he is, Lucifer had no problem using someone else's
destiny to achieve his diabolical agenda. Lucifer whose destiny was in
heaven not earth, cannot assert any rights to the control of the territory
because he is illegitimate. He tells the first lie, committing the very first
act of identity theft, driven by pride and lust conspired to commit
rebellion that was crushed in a flash; *...I beheld Satan as lightning fall
from heaven.* LUKE 10:18. The dissenting angel who was created for heaven,
was motivated to control the territory and the only way he could ever get
that control was to take what he knew was not lawfully his. The destiny
of Adam had been hijacked.

Before I go further, I should point out that your destiny will impact those
close to you and those you love. Adam was a man of great destiny and the
decisions he made had an impact on all mankind. *... Wherefore, as by
one-man sin entered into the world, and death by sin; and so, death
passed upon all men, ...Therefore as by the offence of one judgment
came upon all men to condemnation;* ROMANS 5:1-19. All mankind should
learn that no one can afford to be selfish.

Abraham begat Isaac; and Isaac begat Jacob; and Jacob begat Joseph.
Joseph like Adam had definitive destiny experience. However, because of
Adam's decision to rebel, Joseph's destiny experience will be navigated.
Joseph's brothers were angry and intimidated when Joseph shared a dream
that revealed his destiny. The navigation process begins when the brothers
put Joseph in a pit. *Then they took him and cast him into a pit...*
GENESIS 37:23-24. They thought that getting rid of Joseph would short-circuit
his destiny. Little did they realize that the pit was the first step to secure
the very destiny they wanted to avoid. The navigation continues to
Potiphar's house; *So, Joseph found favor in his sight, and served him.
Then he made him overseer of his house, and all that he had he put*

*under his authority.* GENESIS 39:4. Later to the prison where *...the keeper of the prison committed to Joseph's hand all the prisoners who were in the prison;* GENESIS 39:21-23. The ultimate destination or destiny was the palace of Pharaoh. Favor and influence followed Joseph and now dominion was about to catch up. Joseph wasn't in Egypt by mere brotherly betrayal. Joseph declared to his brothers "*...God sent me before you to preserve life.*" GENESIS 45:5,7. God did what I call divine in vitro fertilization. God took the seed of one nation and placed that seed in the womb of another nation, and after a four-hundred-year gestation period a new nation was born. While Joseph was in Egypt, he built enormous wealth, not for Egypt but to fulfil destiny. *Know of a surety that thy seed shall be a stranger in a land that is not theirs, and shall serve them; and they shall afflict them four hundred years; And also, that nation, whom they shall serve, will I judge: and afterward shall they come out with great substance.* GENESIS 15:13-14. The brothers of Joseph wanted to deny the destiny of Joseph.

Moses like Joseph had a dynamic destiny experience. Before he draws his first breath the attack against him has already been launched. An important fact to remember about seed, it is full of potential, growth, and influence. The Pharaoh of Egypt is after the seed, the potential, the hope, and the very future of Israel. A Levite couple came together to produce and bare a son. Jochebed, the mother of Moses looked at him and knew that he had divine destiny. She saw that he was a goodly child so she hid him. Meanwhile the Pharaoh has recruited the midwives to help him kill babies. *"When you do the duties of a midwife for the Hebrew women, and see them on the birthstools, if it is a son, then you shall kill him..."* EXODUS 1:15 A clear effort to solicit the people to self-destruct. The Pharaoh's approach is the same at the brothers of Joseph, failing to understand that his threatening effort will guarantee the destiny he does not want. *"...Every son who is born you shall cast into the river...."* EXODUS 1:22. *...And the child grew, and she brought him to Pharaoh's daughter, and he became her son. So, she called his name Moses, saying, "Because I drew him out of the water."* EXODUS 2:10. Moses grows up in Pharaoh's own palace as a prince of Egypt, the deliverer that Pharaoh thought he had eliminated. When Moses discovers his not a prince but the son of Hebrew slaves his destiny takes him to Midian. Moses comes face to face with his destiny and the God of his fathers, where he hears the words; *"Come now, therefore, and I will send you to Pharaoh that you may bring My people, the children of Israel, out of Egypt."* ...But

*Moses said to God, "Who am I that I should go to Pharaoh, and that I should bring the children of Israel out of Egypt?"* Moses's attempt to shrink from his true destiny is vain. *So, He said, "I will certainly be with you. And this shall be a sign to you that I have sent you: When you have brought the people out of Egypt, you shall serve God on this mountain." ...And God said to Moses, "I AM WHO I AM." ... "Thus, you shall say to the children of Israel, I AM has sent me to you."* Please type a memo to yourself: "Where ever God should send me and where ever my destiny may lead, my Lord and King will never leave me alone." Pharaoh tried to abort the destiny of Moses.

Many of us grew up hearing the story of David and Goliath. I want to use this story to help enlighten us regarding David's destiny. David, the youngest of the eight sons of Jesse, was a shepherd who was proficient in feeding and protecting sheep. He was never groomed to be a king or a man armed for war. Goliath was described as a Philistine giant, a man of combat who knew how to wage warfare. Goliath was known for bullying, threatening, and taunting Israel. As the story goes David and Goliath came face to face in a stressed insurmountable encounter. It appeared that David was outmatched. In his human wisdom, the King thought to give his armor to David. An old testament version of a bad man with a gun versus a good man with a gun. *...David said unto Saul, I cannot go with these; for I have not proved them. And David put them off him. ...he took his staff in his hand, and chose him five smooth stones out of the brook, and put them in a shepherd's bag which he had, even in a scrip; and his sling was in his hand: and he drew near to the Philistine.* 1 SAMUEL 17:39-40. David knew it would be inefficient to use a weapon he was never trained with or a weapon he never used. David knew that if God delivered him from a lion and a bear surely God could deliver him from the Philistine. David is destined to become the King who thinks like a King, *after God's own heart.* David's destiny is to be the King who knew how to shepherd and the King who understood the power of worship. David was dismissed with disregard to his destiny.

*In the beginning was the Word, and the Word was with God, and the Word was God. The same was in the beginning with God. All things were made by him; and without him was not anything made that was made.* JOHN 1:1-3. Jesus was recognized as the master teacher, or rabbi in the New Testament. In the old testament God declares that He is the great I AM, *...thou say unto the children of Israel, I AM hath sent me unto you.*

EXODUS 3:13-14. In the book of Revelations, He says; *...I am Alpha and Omega, the beginning and the end. I will give unto him that is athirst of the fountain of the water of life freely. He that overcometh shall inherit all things; and I will be his God, and he shall be my son.* REVELATION 21:6-7. As I pondered how to write this paragraph, I was a little overwhelmed. Where can I find the words to explain the destiny of Jesus? I was then reminded what Jesus once said to Peter, *"...flesh and blood has not revealed this to you, but My Father who is in heaven.* MATTHEW 16:17. The Holy Spirit came to take me on a spiritual mental journey through the scriptures. I was reminded of *...a child is born and a son is given and the government shall be upon his shoulder; and his name shall be called Wonderful, Counselor, The mighty God, The everlasting Father, The Prince of Peace".* ISAIAH 9:6. I begin to think in the context of the Son of Man, the Word made flesh. *...the Word became flesh and dwelt among us, and we beheld His glory, the glory as of the only begotten of the Father, full of grace and truth.* JOHN 1:14. Jesus came to Judea as a man.

Jesus was born as a man; *Now the birth of Jesus Christ was as follows: After His mother Mary was betrothed to Joseph, before they came together, she was found with child of the Holy Spir*it. MATTHEW 1:18. He was baptized and anointed as a man. He was tempted as a man. He prayed as a man. He walked to and fro as a man. He was betrayed and arrested as a man. He agonized as a man. He stood as a guilty man. He thirsted as a man. He was crucified as a guilty man. He bled and died as a man. The destiny of Jesus, as the son of man, was to restore the system that was hijacked by a rough agent. Jesus reestablished His Kingdom Government as He redeemed the man who was created to have dominion; *God said, "Let Us make man in Our image, according to Our likeness; let them have dominion..."* GENESIS 1:26-28.

Jesus never came to establish any religion of any kind. Jesus came to redeem man redeeming the system that was usurped. *For if by one man's offence death reigned by one; much more they which receive abundance of grace and of the gift of righteousness shall reign in life by one, Jesus Christ. Therefore, as by the offence of one judgment came upon all men to condemnation; even so by the righteousness of one the free gift came upon all men unto justification of life. For as by one man's disobedience many were made sinners, so by the obedience of one shall many be made righteous.* ROMANS 5:17-19. He came to reestablish his government authorizing his *ekklesia* to influence the earth. *...Jesus said unto them, I must preach the kingdom of God to other cities also: for therefore am I sent.* LUKE 4:43.

Think on this, God created mankind to have dominion on the earth. God gave mankind access to all resources on the earth. God created a habitation and placed mankind in His presence. Mankind was then fortified with the Spirit of God. Mankind has always been well equipped to bring Heaven to Earth. Remember *Thy kingdom come, thy will be done in earth, as it is in heaven...* MATTHEW 6:10. While religion has taught us to long for Heaven, we should manifest Heaven here on earth through the Kingdom of God. We are the yeast of influence, the culture, the righteousness, and the likeness of the Kingdom of Heaven. Remember as well from the book of Revelation, John said; *And I saw a new heaven and a new earth...:* REVELATION 21:1.

The destiny of the Son of Man was made secure from the beginning. His destiny could not be hijacked, denied, disregarded, or aborted. Jesus came to redeem the man, to reestablish the Kingdom of God in the earth. Now the man can walk in true destiny and God given dominion.

# Kingdom Integrity

## Integrity Matters

☐PSALMS 145:8-10, 17

I n the Genesis story an attack was launched on the integrity of God. An attempt to persuade man that God can't be trusted and will let the man down and leave him hanging. *...the serpent said to the woman, "You will not surely die. For God knows that in the day you eat of it your eyes will be opened and you will be like God, knowing good and evil."* GENESIS 3:1-5. This dialog gave birth to an adversarial relationship between God and man. There is a spirit of discord and we can see it manifested in many different ways around the world. We know it as protest and dissent, rioting, racial or social injustice. No matter what we call it, it is designed to undermine our relationship with divine authority. Is it any wonder why relationships with authority are adversarial?

The citizens living in the kingdom need to know that they can trust their King. From the beginning of creation man's continued existence has been secured by the integrity of God. God made a covenant with Abraham and Abraham's seed. When Ishmael and his mother were dying in the desert God heard the lad crying in the desert. God saved the boy and his mother. Ishmael was not the child of promise, but he was the seed of Abraham. God made sure Ishmael did not die in the dessert. *And God heard the voice of the lad; ...Fear not; for God hath heard the voice of the lad where he is. ...Arise, lift up the lad, and hold him in thine hand; for I* *will make him a great nation...*GENESIS 21:17-19. God would not let the child die. God protected His word, His reputation, and His integrity!

The integrity of God guarantees that you wake up to a shining sun daily. Clouds bear witness that the waters are still dividing. The next time you feel the ground move under your feet remember the integrity of God. *...God said, Let the waters under the heaven be gathered together unto one place, and let the dry land appear: and it was so.* GENESIS 1:10; The tectonic plates have been shifting ever since. Apples still grow on apple trees. Dolphins still live at sea. The oceans and the seas are faithful to their boundaries and after hurricanes strike against the dry land to create storm surge, the waters recede. Our King is always the same and he will always protect his name. *Jesus Christ the same yesterday, and today, and forever.* HEBREWS 13:8

The elders of Israel gathered themselves together, and came to Samuel to complain about the judges in Beersheba. The judges lost the trust of the people because of corruption, bribes, and a lust for money. Clearly the men operated without any integrity. The Lord spoke to Samuel to alert him that the Elders *...have not rejected thee, but they have rejected me, that I should not reign over them.* 1 SAMUEL 8:7. The Lord knew that the rulers of the earth would abuse. The Lord knew that the men had no integrity. The tyrant will have no interest in the wellbeing of the people. The despot will use his power while he enriches his own life. The rulers of the earth will be oppressive, wasteful and exploitive. So, the Lord posted a disclaimer. *He will take your sons and appoint them for his own chariots and to be his horsemen, ...He will take your daughters to be perfumers, ...He will take a tenth of your grain and your vintage and give it to his officers and servants. And he will take your male servants, your female servants, your finest young men, ...and put them to his work.* 1 SAMUEL 8:11-17. The elders were warned! Whether its communism, socialism, or even democracy the people must guard themselves against men who act with no integrity. The citizens will protest that they can't trust their government. The security of the people will be at risk when the ruler is found to be dishonest and deceitful. No man wants to live where the rulers have no integrity.

The roman guard who witnessed the resurrection firsthand, reported what they saw to the chief priest. *While the women were on their way, some of the guard went into the city and reported to the chief priests everything that had happened.* MATTHEW 28:11. The guard had to report that the dead man they were guarding had walked out of the tomb. Try listing that on your military resume. *While they had assembled with the elders and consulted together, they gave a large sum of money to the soldiers, saying, tell them, His disciples came at night and stole Him away while we slept. And if this comes to the governor's ears, we will appease him and make you secure. So, they took the money and did as they were instructed...* MATTHEW 28:12-14. Admitting that you were asleep while guarding the tomb of a dead man is not something to boast about. The chief priest gave large sums of money to the soldiers to perpetuate a lie. Taking money to lie is a textbook description of *"men of no integrity"*.

Men with no integrity want to live in opulence and luxury while they watch the citizens languish. But the King of the Kingdom isn't like that. David said it best; *I've never seen the righteous forsaken...* PSALMS 37:25 *...the kingdom of heaven is like to a grain of mustard seed, which a man took, and sowed in his field: Which indeed is the least of all seeds: but when it is grown, it is the greatest among herbs, and becomes a tree, so that the birds of the air come and lodge in the branches thereof.* MATTHEW 13:31-32. The resources of the Kingdom are without limits. The Lord's resources can't be depleted.

We are, without fail, able to trust God's integrity because the Lord is immutable, *...to shew unto the heirs of promise the immutability of his counsel, confirmed it by an oath: That by two immutable things, in which it was impossible for God to lie, ...we have as an anchor of the soul, both sure and steadfast, ...* HEBREWS 6:16-20. God will never violate his own name or his reputation. *Thus, saith the Lord God; I do not this for your sakes, O house of Israel, but for mine holy name's sake;* There are times when we forget the preciousness His name. The times when we try to blame him for our bad situation. We force God to ask us why are we wroth, what happen to your smile? However, the Lord will not join us in the destruction His reputation. Even if He has to save us for his own name's sake. *...I will sanctify my great name,* we join the heathen to mock his name, *...which was profaned among the heathen, which ye have profaned in the midst of them;* but God will have the last laugh, *the heathen shall know that I am the Lord, ...Not for your sakes do I this, saith the Lord God. ... But for mine holy name's sake.* EZEKIEL 36:22-26; 32. God is committed to the protection of his name, his image, and his reputation no matter how wicked man may become. The Lord is faithful, we owe a lot of our redemption to the integrity of His faithfulness.

I need to know I won't be abandoned by the King who loves me. All my questions were answered when Jesus went to the cross. His death said that He will never exploit me. So, I lift my hands like a child to my Father to hear that He loves me. Great Is Thy Faithfulness is a popular hymn written as an expression of God's unchanging integrity.

*Great is Thy faithfulness, O God my Father;*

*There is no shadow of turning with Thee;*

*Thou change not, thy compassions, they fail not;*

*As Thou hast been, thou forever will be.*

*Summer and winter and springtime and harvest,*

*Sun, moon and stars in their courses above*

*Join with all nature in manifold witness*

*To Thy great faithfulness, mercy and love.*

*Strength for today and bright hope for tomorrow,*

*Blessings all mine, with ten thousand beside!*

*Pardon for sin and a peace that endures*

*Thine own dear presence to cheer and to guide;*

*Great is Thy faithfulness!*

*Great is Thy faithfulness!*

*Morning by morning new mercies I see.*

*All I have needed Thy hand hath provided;*

*Great is Thy faithfulness, Lord, unto me!*

*--Thomas O. Chisholm*

***The Lord is righteous in all his ways, and holy in all his works.*** PSALMS 145:17. Pay close attention to the words ***righteous, holy,*** and ***all***. God's integrity is whole, complete, and full. Isn't it great to have a King whom you can trust without fail? Our King will not abandon us or leave us in our storm. Our King will not leave us to die in the desert. Our King will shepherd us and stay with us as we walk through the valley and the shadow of death. Our King will prepare a table in the presence of our enemies. Our King will not be intimidated by the antagonism of our enemies, and they will stumble to fall. Our King has promised that we shall be with Him in paradise. The integrity of the King is the warranty that secures our redemption and our peace. The integrity of the King guarantees that His righteousness will not fail. ***The fear of man brings a snare, but whoever trusts in the Lord shall be safe.*** PROVERBS 29:25.

# Kingdom Righteousness

Righteousness Matters!

📖 ROMANS 5:1-19

The American constitution guarantees each citizen equal rights and equal justice under the law. Civil rights to equal rights to freedom of choice will give voice to citizens who have a thirst and a hunger for justice. Victims of spousal abuse, sexual abuse, child abuse, and police brutality are waiting for predators to be held accountable by the government. The government must make sure that all violators understand the consequences for those who have no regard for law and order. The constitution is a contract between the government and the governed citing declarations of equality, justice, and rights. All governments must establish a system of justice to maintain law and order. Jesus affirms one of the benefits of the Kingdom; *Blessed are those who hunger and thirst for righteousness, for they shall be filled.* MATTHEW 5:6. We should remember the priority as well given to us by Jesus; *...seek ye first the kingdom of God, and his righteousness;* MATTHEW 6:33.

Let the record show. God created man and gave the man dominion over the earth. God then gave the man access to all the resources of the earth. However, unfettered dominion and access will open the door to undisciplined control. The earth was created with order. Therefore, the earth will not be left to the dominion of a man who would be disobedient, seditious, rebellious, or aimless. The earth was created with order, there will be law, order, and boundaries. The creator, who had sovereign creative ownership rights, fully expected that creation will respect boundaries and follow righteousness.

Meanwhile later the same day, it was reported that man was stalked by a criminal known for spreading disinformation. AKA the prince of darkness. The prince of darkness convinced the female, who convinced the male that God could not be trusted. They were persuaded that the boundary was a ploy used by God to keep man from becoming who they really are. As this crime was exposed a divine subpoena was issued, *...And the Lord God called unto Adam, and said unto him, where art thou?* -GENESIS 3:9. The male and the female are compelled to give testimony giving evidence before the judge in open court. Also appearing in the court before the Judge was the plaintiff, identified as righteousness. This plaintiff, righteousness, appeared to demand justice. The criminal, the defendant must be held accountable. Those who act against righteousness must learn that there will be consequences when showing such disregard for the boundary, *the wages of sin is death.*

**Righteous Lives Matter!!!** The word righteousness appears about 306 times in the KJV bible. *...seek ye first the kingdom of God, and his righteousness;* MATTHEW 6:33. This particular priority given to us by Jesus makes it very clear the significance of *right standing status* with the divine Lord. If man is going to honor the covenant agreement, if man is going to keep the divine fellowship and relationship the man must abide by the law. As the case against man was adjudicated and all the testimonies giving evidence of the violation were heard, it was clear that man lost *right standing status.* The man was driven from the presence of God. He will now know toil, sweat, sorrow and enmity. *...Unto Adam also and to his wife did the LORD God make coats of skins, and clothed them.* GENESIS 3:21. Man suffered the cost of disobedience, or did he? It was clear that there was blood to cover the man, however it was not the blood of the man. Righteousness wasn't requited and was not satisfied. Righteousness will continue to demand justice. *...Cain talked with Abel his brother: and it came to pass, when they were in the field, that Cain rose up against Abel his brother, and slew him. And the LORD said* *unto Cain, where is Abel thy brother? And he said, I know not: Am I my brother's keeper? And he said, what hast thou done? the voice of thy brother's blood crieth unto me from the ground.* GENESIS 4:8. Righteousness will continue to demand justice.

A dental patient makes a visit to the dentist, for dental surgery. After the dental extraction the patient leaves the dentist office with two medications. An opioid, and an antibiotic. The opioid is used to help the patient endure the suffering and alleviate the pain. The patient is instructed to apply the opioid only as needed. However, the antibiotic will bring about the healing of the wound. The patient will have to apply the antibiotic until "*it is finished.*" Pain medication may relieve the pain but it will not eliminate the cause of the pain. Mitigation may make everyone feel good temporarily. This mitigation may cover up the evidence for a time. Mitigation may even manifest mercy. However, mitigation cannot testify "*it is finished.*" The **coats of skins** only alleviated the suffering and the pain. ***Unto Adam also and to his wife did the LORD God make coats of skins and clothed them.*** GENESIS 3:21. Coats of skins will need to be applied as needed until the blood of a man is applied. …***For what the law could not do in that it was weak through the flesh, God did by sending His own Son in the likeness of sinful flesh, on account of sin: He condemned sin in the flesh…***ROMANS 8:3. Righteousness wasn't requited and continues to demand justice.

God used the seed of Abraham to create a nation. The seed became a family. The family became a tribe. The tribe became a nation. All nations are structured with a system of justice established to guarantee that criminals are held accountable for the crimes they commit. While the man through rebellion destroyed the divine fellowship, God covered the man with coats of skins to save the relationship. This relationship will need the priesthood to continue.

The priesthood became a mitigation and the go-between. The priests were necessary because God was separated from the fallen man. God ordained that certain men who were ritually cleansed in a special way should approach him on behalf of the people. They would make offerings of sacrifice to God which symbolically atoned, or paid for the man's sin but it was still not the blood of the man. The priests officiated at many offerings, the sin offering, the guilt offering, the red heifer, and various purification rituals. However, righteousness will continue to demand justice.

The act of giving up one thing for another may appease, but it will not be sufficient for peace. That, a lamb or a bull should be offered for the blood of a man is not enough to heal the wound of disobedience. The offender will have to offer sacrifice over and over and over again. In religion sacrifice is nothing more than an opioid. Ever since the rebellion, man has been trying to regain the validation of his Father. Religion and rituals will never be enough to re-establish validation. The only way man will be restored is through requited righteousness. *...For the kingdom of God is not meat and drink; but righteousness, and peace, and joy in the Holy Ghost.* ROMANS 14:17. "*No Justice, No Peace!*" is more than a mantra or movement, it is the foundation of a fundamental truth. Righteousness demands justice and man will have no peace or joy until righteousness has been requited.

To call Jesus the Lamb of God identifies "*the lamb*" to be significantly different from any other lamb, dove, or heifer. There are at least 85 KJV passages that mentions the lamb that refers to a sacrifice. The priest had to come back year after year because no common lamb could require righteousness. Jesus is much more than a sacrifice. Jesus is a true substitution, in other words a *propitiation. ...He made Him who knew no sin to be sin for us, that we might become the righteousness of God in Him.* 2 CORINTHIANS 5:21. Jesus came to the court room to stand in front of the Judge and offered himself for the guilty man. Jesus understood the offence, He understood the penalty, and He understood the suffering. Jesus exchanges his innocence for your guilt and shame. Still Jesus tapped the guilty man on the shoulder and told him *"I got this"*. Making Jesus more than a mere sacrifice. Jesus is the offering and the offeror who accepts the offering terminating the power of revocation that the offeror legally owned. This makes Jesus the ultimate gift; *...God so loved the world, that he gave his only begotten Son...* JOHN 3:16. Jesus was the only *"lamb"* who declared *"it is finished!"*. This declaration announced the end of all mitigation.

God gave his only begotten son. That one gift is the most extraordinary demonstration of love in the history of the earth. However, we should never ever forget that the crucifixion is equally one powerful act of justice and righteousness. According to the allegory found in the book of Hosea. Gomer went after false lovers only to be *redeemed* by her husband. *...I bought her to me for fifteen pieces of silver, and for a homer of barley, and an half homer of barley: And I said unto her, Thou shalt abide for me many days; thou shalt not play the harlot, and thou shalt not be for another man: so will I also be for thee.* HOSEA 3:1-3. Jesus is the offeror in this divine transaction making righteousness a significant priority. The Kingdom will not prosper without righteousness. This may sound like a cliché but there must be law and order. Take a fish out of the water and the fish will die. Lock a bird in a cage and the bird will suffer. After the storm surge strikes, the water will recede. When the man is driven from the presence of God the man will die. There will be no fellowship between righteousness and unrighteousness, there will be no communion of light with darkness. We can never say enough; *...For the kingdom of God is not meat and drink; but righteousness, and peace, and joy in the Holy Ghost.* ROMANS 14:17. *"No Justice, No Peace! No Joy"*

The blood of the Son of man, requites righteousness. *Therefore, being justified by faith, we have peace with God through our Lord Jesus Christ: By whom also we have access by faith into this grace wherein we stand, and rejoice in hope of the glory of God.... God commended his love toward us, in that, while we were yet sinners, Christ died for us. Much more then, being now justified by his blood, we shall be saved from wrath through him. For if, when we were enemies, we were reconciled to God by the death of his Son, much more, being reconciled, we shall be saved by his life. And not only so, but we also joy in God through our Lord Jesus Christ, by whom we have now received the atonement. Wherefore, as by one-man sin entered into the world, and death by sin; and so, death passed upon all men, for that all have sinned: ...Therefore as by the offence of one judgment came upon all men to condemnation; even so by the righteousness of one the free gift came upon all men unto justification of life. For as by one man's disobedience many were made sinners, so by the obedience of one shall many be made righteous.* ROMANS 5:1-19

*...For what the law could not do in that it was weak through the flesh, God did by sending His own Son in the likeness of sinful flesh, on account of sin: He condemned sin in the flesh...*ROMANS 8:3

*But now in Christ Jesus ye who sometimes were far off are made nigh by the blood of Christ. For he is our peace, who hath made both one, and hath broken down the middle wall of partition between us; Having abolished in his flesh the enmity, even the law of commandments contained in ordinances; for to make in himself of twain one new man, so making peace; And that he might reconcile both unto God in one body by the cross, having slain the enmity thereby: And came and preached peace to you which were afar off, and to them that were nigh. For through him we both have access by one Spirit unto the Father. Now therefore ye are no more strangers and foreigners, but fellow citizens with the saints, and of the household of God;* EPHESIANS 2:13-19.

<u>Righteous Lives Matter!!!</u>

| | | |
|---|---|---|
| Righteousness | KJV | 306 |
| Righteous | KJV | 238 |

# Kingdom Legitimacy

## Thou Art the CHRIST

☐MATTHEW 16:13-18

The most powerful relationship of the Kingdom is the relationship between the father and the son. The father son relationship establishes birthrights, entitlements, privileges, legacy, inheritance, and legitimacy. God said, *"Let them have dominion."* GENESIS 1:26-28. Male and female created he *them* is the declaration that we are all sons. We call God Father. All sons seek and pursue validation from fathers. Adam was validated by the Father. *...God saw everything that he had made, and, behold, it was very good.* GENESIS 1:31. Adam lost his identity through disobedience. Jesus was conceived, the only begotten son. Jesus is validated by his Father. *...This is my beloved Son, in whom I am well pleased.* MATTHEW 3:17 *...Thou art my beloved Son, in whom I am well pleased.* MARK 1:11. Jesus was obedient unto death. Jesus is the Christ seated on the right hand of his Father. Legitimate authority can only be conferred by the Father. Any authority not established by the Father will be regarded as illegitimate.

Lucifer, who was created for heaven and not for earth, cannot assert any rights to the control of the earth because he is illegitimate. Lucifer wanted to control the world and the only way he could ever get control of the world was to steal what he knew was not lawfully his. He proceeded to establish his illegitimate government, asserting illegal and counterfeit control of the world.

Being the thief that he is, he tells the first lie, committing the very first act of identity theft. Lucifer has no legal position to make any claims to rights, entitlements, or privileges.

Satan is called the prince of darkness for a reason; *…The god of this world hath blinded the minds of them which believe not, lest the light of the glorious gospel of Christ, who is the image of God, should shine unto them.* 2 CORINTHIANS 4:2. Illegitimate leaders are dangerous because they govern with no integrity. The lack of integrity sets up environments that are given to exploitation, despotism, and injustice. By their nature oppressors are psychotic and paranoid and they are driven by fear and insecurity. When the psychosis advances to delusion, the men who tell lies begin to believe the lies the men tell. In an effort to replace God they set themselves up as powerful rulers. This psychosis poses a danger to the citizens and makes their lives insecure and unstable. God conferred legitimate authority, creating man in His image and likeness, fortifying man with His spirit; *let them have dominion…*Man was fortified with legitimate authority; *but he did eat…*Satan hijacked and assumed false identity asserting illegitimate authority.

Man, through rebellion forfeited legitimate authority, subsequently he was driven from the presence of God. *Therefore, the Lord God sent him forth from the garden …he drove out the man; …*GENESIS 3:23-24. When man lost the presence of God, he lost dominion, he lost identity, and he lost legitimate authority. Man was reduced to manual living. *…Then to Adam He said, because you have heeded the voice of your wife, and have eaten from the tree of which I commanded you, saying, 'You shall not eat of it': Cursed is the ground for your sake; in toil you shall eat of it all the days of your life. …In the sweat of your face, you shall eat bread …*GENESIS 3:17-19. Ever since that day man has been trying to regain the validation of his Father. The only way man can regain established validation of his Father is through requited righteousness.

*...For the kingdom of God is not meat and drink; but righteousness, and peace, and joy in the Holy Ghost.* ROMANS 14:17. "*No Justice, No Peace!*" Righteousness demands justice and man will have no joy or peace until righteousness has been requited.

The psychology of the thief is to assume ownership of what he has stolen. This thinking sets up the delusion that the thief has legal right and discretion to award or restrict that which he does not legitimately own. *...And the devil said to Him, all this authority I will give you, and their glory; for this has been delivered to me, and I give it to whomever I wish. Therefore, if you will worship before me, all will be yours.* LUKE 4:6-7. Let us be clear, the thief has no legitimate authority to corrupt the Lord. Let us be equally clear, satan was not confused about who Jesus is or his legitimacy. Satan's delusion forced him to challenge the Lord regarding his legitimacy. *If you are the Son of God, command this stone to become bread.* LUKE 4:3. Make no mistake *...All things were made by him; and without him was not anything made that was made.* JOHN 1:3.

Jesus asked his disciples a question to which everyone wanted an answer. *... Whom do men say that I the Son of man am? ... Whom say ye that I am ...Then Peter answered... "Thou art the Christ, the Son of the living God".* MATTHEW 16:13-18. The answer to that question is imperative because legitimate governments are established by legitimate sons. *Jesus answered and said to him, "Blessed are you, Simon Bar-Jonah, for flesh and blood has not revealed this to you, but My Father who is in heaven.* MATTHEW 16:17

Once again God validates His Son. Satan can never assert legitimate authority because he is not a son. We used to sing a song; "*God gave me a song the angels can't sing*". Satan can't sing our song because satan is not a son. Satan is the son of perdition! Christ being the Son of God is the anointed and legitimate King. The Son will establish the legitimate government in the earth...*a child is born and a son is given and the government shall be upon his shoulder; and his name shall be called Wonderful, Counselor, The mighty God, The everlasting Father, The Prince of Peace".* ISAIAH 9:6. *...If you had known me, you would have* *known My Father also; He who has seen me has seen the Father; ...Do you not believe that I am in the Father, and the Father in Me? The words that I speak to you I do not speak on my own authority; but the Father who dwells in me......I am in the Father and the Father in Me* JOHN 14:7-11.

The son comes with vested authority; ...***when the fullness of the time was come, God sent forth his Son...***GALATIANS 4:4. In the Genesis story Adam could have responded; *I am created in my Father's image and in my Father's likeness, I am just like my Father fortified with my Father's breath. I speak with the authority of my Father who gave me dominion.*

When King George V, died in 1936 the Prince of Wales, became King of England, Edward VIII. However, the new king abdicated and forfeited all of his legitimate sovereign rights over England, losing all of his property. Edward VIII was re-named Duke of Windsor. The Duke could not stay in England. When Edward VIII abdicated, he was divested of all legitimate authority and all rights. The Duke could no longer assert any legitimate rights while he was in a foreign territory. The Duke died in France.

The death of Christ restores man's legitimacy through redemption. Through the loss of identity man has lost legitimacy but he is able to regain the God vested legitimacy through the redemptive work of Christ on the cross. The legitimacy is rightfully ours because of the eternal inheritance. When the prodigal son returned to his father ... ***the father said to his servants, bring forth the best robe, and put it on him; and put a ring on his hand, and shoes on his feet.*** LUKE 15:22. The father restored the son's legitimate sovereign peace.

Jesus Christ restores legitimate authority; ***all power is given unto me in heaven and in earth.*** Jesus is able to do it, Jesus did do it, and it was His to do. ...***Go ye therefore, ...In*** his ***name*** we ***shall cast out devils;*** we ***shall speak with new tongues;*** we ***shall take up serpents; and if*** we ***drink any deadly thing, it shall not hurt*** us...MARK 16:17- 18.

We are charged to do it, we must do it, and it is ours to do.

*He is the Mediator of the new covenant, by means of death, for the redemption of the transgressions under the first covenant, that those who are called may receive the promise of the eternal inheritance.* HEBREWS 9:15. *Thou art no more a servant, but a son; and if a son, then an heir of God through Christ.* GALATIANS 4:7. *But as many as received him, to them gave he power to become the sons of God,* JOHN 1:12. *Beloved, now are we the sons of God.* 1 JOHN 3:2. *...For as many as are led by the Spirit of God, they are the sons of God.... ROMANS 8:14. ...a son is given and the government shall be upon his shoulder; and his name shall be called Wonderful, Counselor, The mighty God, The everlasting Father, The Prince of Peace".* ISAIAH 9:6.

*Therefore, being justified by faith, we have peace with God through our Lord Jesus Christ: By whom also we have access by faith into this grace wherein we stand, and rejoice in hope of the glory of God. ...being now justified by his blood, we shall be saved from wrath through him. ...when we were enemies, we were reconciled to God by the death of his Son, much more, being reconciled, we shall be saved by his life. And not only so, but we also joy in God through our Lord Jesus Christ, by whom we have now received the atonement. Wherefore, as by one-man sin entered into the world, and death by sin; and so, death passed upon all men, ...Therefore as by the offence of one judgment came upon all men to condemnation; even so by the righteousness of one the free gift came upon all men unto justification of life. For as by one man's disobedience many were made sinners, so by the obedience of one shall many be made righteous.* ROMANS 5:1-19.

I am fortified in the knowledge that as a legitimate son any attempt by an illegal government will be defeated with God inspired authority. *The Lord is my light and my salvation; ...the Lord is the strength of my life; ...When the wicked, even mine enemies and my foes, came upon me to eat up my flesh, they stumbled and fell.* PSALMS 27:1-2.

Affirmed by and secured through the redemptive work of Christ on the cross I am authorized to manifest God given influence as a legitimate son. *...Come, you who are blessed by my Father; take your inheritance, the kingdom prepared for you since the creation of the world.* MATTHEW 25:34. Only legitimate sons have legitimate authority.

# Kingdom Influence

The Finger of God!

☐MATTHEW 13:33

T*he kingdom of heaven is like leaven, which a woman took and hid in three measures of meal till it was all leavened.*

MATTHEW 13:33.During the English Reformation Henry VIII sanctioned the complete destruction of shrines of the Catholic Church. England's remaining monasteries were all dissolved, and their property transferred to the crown. The king had to make sure that there were no signs of the old Catholic Church in an effort to establish the Church of England. The Act of Supremacy was established to declare that Henry was the Supreme Head of the Church of England. He was driven to remove anything catholic or any images thereof.

*In the beginning, God created the heaven and the earth. And the earth was without form, and void; and darkness was upon the face of the deep. And the Spirit of God moved upon the face of the waters.*
GENESIS 1:1-2.

The Kingdom of God is the influence of the Kingdom of Heaven on the earth. The very first Person on the earth was the Holy Spirit and when he came his influence undoubtedly brought about change. Before the Holy Spirit came, the earth *was without form,* it *was void,* and it *was dark.* The Holy Spirit arrived and he brought order, structure, and efficiency. The priority of the Holy Spirit is to administer the will of the King until the distant territory looks just like the original kingdom. The Holy Spirit's priority is to teach the King's will, his values, his ethics, and his culture so that the citizens begin to talk like the King, walk like the King, live just like the King. God wants the influence of the Kingdom of Heaven to extend to the earth through the Kingdom of God. The visible Kingdom of God should look just like the invisible Kingdom of Heaven. Remember... *Thy kingdom come. Thy will be done in earth, as it is in heaven...* MATTHEW 6:10

*The Lord God planted a garden eastward in Eden, and there He put the man whom He had formed.* GENESIS 2:8. When a kingdom takes over a distant territory the King will *put* an administrator in place fortified with His influence to make sure that the values and culture of the original kingdom are demonstrated in the distant territory. The man is fortified with influence and then the man is put into position to assert the influence of the Kingdom of Heaven through the Kingdom of God. God called Abraham from his home and showed him the land that he planned to give him. ...*Lift your eyes now and look from the place where you are— northward, southward, eastward, and westward; for all the land which you see I give to you and your descendants forever.* GENESIS 13:14-15. Then God does what can be called full disclosure. He told Abraham about all the other people already living in the land. ...*The Kenites, the Kenizzites, the Kadmonites, the Hittites, the Perizzites, ...the Rephaims, ...the Amorites, ...the Canaanites, ...the Girgashites, and...the Jebusites.* GENESIS 15:19-21. All these people were already living in the land with their own set of values and their own set of beliefs. A land already under government, ideology, and influence.

From Haran to Mt. Sinai, from Abraham to Moses, the people have been exposed to other peoples and other lands. There were many opportunities to acquire and assimilate cultural behaviors that are foreign to God. Haran, Sodom, and Egypt are filled with many different morals and cultures. Amorites, Hittites, Canaanites, and Jebusites filled the land with different customs, behaviors, and influences. God's plan for his people was to keep them from the strange gods, and practices. Consider this; God separates Abram from his father and his country to separate him from old culture and influence. Then God restricts Abram from adopting the cultures or the influence that are already in the territory with the expressed purpose to bring the territory under the influence of the Kingdom of God. *...You shall not bow down to their gods, nor serve them, nor do according to their works;* EXODUS 23:24. God's intention was to fill the land with His people, His culture, and His influence. Abraham was not a squatter, a tourist, or a visitor. The new nation will not assimilate to the prevailing cultures. The new nation will have to displace the old influence.

God calls on Abram to maintain His kingdom influence on the earth. Abraham begets Isaac, Isaac begets Jacob, and Jacob begets Judah and his brothers, and these twelve brothers become what we know as the Tribes of Israel. The territory will be divided into twelve provinces. God made a promise to Abraham that his descendants would become a nation; *...Now the Lord had said to Abram: Get out of your country, from your family and from your father's house, to a land that I will show you. I will make you a great nation* ...GENESIS 12:1-2. The nation will need a government. No nation on earth exists without a government. The government will bring order. The mandate for the tribes is to take the territory and influence that territory with the Kingdom of God.

*...Speak to the children of Israel and say to them: When you have crossed the Jordan into the land of Canaan, then you shall drive out all the inhabitants of the land from before you.* After Israel takes the territory and displaces the influence, they have to destroy any vestiges of the old influence. The new nation cannot leave any signs of the previous influence; *destroy all their engraved stones, destroy all their molded images, and demolish all their high places; you shall dispossess the inhabitants of the land and dwell in it, for I have given you the land to possess.* NUMBERS 33:50--53.

As the nation grows and transitions God does what I call divine *in vitro fertilization*. God takes the seed of one nation and places that seed in the womb of another nation, and after a four-hundred-year gestation period a new nation is born. Joseph and his brothers don't just end up in Egypt. God will keep his promise to Abraham by saving the seed from pre-mature dispersion. One of these brothers will have to go to Egypt first. Joseph is in Egypt to establish influence and Egypt will never be the same again.

*Joseph called the name of the firstborn Manasseh: God has made me forget all my toil and all my father's house. And the name of the second he called Ephraim: For God has caused me to be fruitful in the land of my affliction.* GENESIS 41:50-52. Egypt didn't get into Joseph as much as Joseph got into Egypt. Joseph was never going to get back to Canaan and he thinks he will never see his father again. Still, he needs to be faithful to the mandate. Joseph will learn that fruitfulness is not dependent on geography. Fruitfulness of Joseph is evidence of his influence.

*Every place that the sole of your foot shall tread upon, that have I given unto you...* JOSHUA 1:3. After the death of Moses God promised Joshua that everywhere he planted his feet would belong to the nation. To establish a divine pattern preparing the territory, influence will precede you. By the time Joshua gets to Jericho, Rahab was already so influenced by what she heard about Joshua and his God that she hid Joshua from the King of Jericho. Rahab was so persuaded that she was willing to put herself and her family at risk. *...I know that the Lord hath given you the land, ...For we have heard how the Lord dried up the water of the Red sea for you, ...and what ye did unto the two kings of the Amorites, that were on the other side Jordan, Sihon and Og, whom ye utterly destroyed. And as soon as we had heard these things, our hearts did melt, ...the Lord your God, he is God in heaven above, and in earth beneath,* JOSHUA 2:9-11. *... But she had brought them up to the roof of the house, and hid them with the stalks of flax, which she had laid in order upon the roof.* JOSHUA 2:4-6. This one strategic act helped Joshua take Jericho.

Naomi was such an influence on Ruth that when Naomi decided to leave Moab and return to Judah, Ruth refused to be left behind. Ruth was a Moabite. She was born and raised in paganism. The Moabites were known for immorality, seduction, lust and incest. The priests of Moab were powerful and cruel, and they served a hodge-podge of gods. However, when left with a choice Ruth chose to follow Naomi to live with her, to live with her God and her people. ... *I will go; and where thou lodgest, I will lodge: thy people shall be my people, and thy God my God:* RUTH 1:16. Subsequently Ruth was married to Boaz, and became the mother of Obed, the grandfather of David. Because of the powerful influence, Ruth, a Gentile can be listed among the maternal progenitors of Jesus. Ruth came to know the living God of Israel through the *redemptive* act of a kinsman-redeemer. If any book in the bible illustrates grace and the divine plan of redemption, it is the book of Ruth.

Fast-forward to the day when Jesus asks his disciples a very important question; *...whom do men say that I the Son of man am... who do you say that I am? ...Peter answered and said to Him, you are the Christ. the Son of the living God* MATTHEW 16:13. Jesus then responds as only a King would; *...on this rock I will build my ekklesia ...*Ekklesia is not a religious body. However, ekklesia is the assembly of Christ, a civil body empowered to influence the earth with the Kingdom of God. *...He breathed on them, and said to them, Receive the Holy Spirit.* JOHN 20:22. The Kingdom will make an impact with the will, the values, the culture, and the language of the King. Christ empowered the twelve disciples with the Holy Ghost and authorized them to impact the earth with God's will. The ekklesia, fortified with the Holy Spirit, will impact the territory and His government will increase. *Of the increase of His government and peace there will be no end...* ISAIAH 9:7

After the resurrection, the disciples were commissioned...*And he said unto them, go ye into all the world, and preach the gospel to every creature.* MARK 16:15. Jesus established an ekklesia, not a religion. The ekklesia has a mandate to go to all of the world systems with kingdom influence. The ekklesia will engage while religion divides and isolates. If we are going to influence, we will have to engage. There will be no impact until the yeast is mixed in with the loaf. Jesus instructed the ekklesia to *go into.* We need Kingdom citizens *in* congress to influence legislation with kingdom concepts and principles. Separation of church and state does not apply to the Kingdom. Separation works to prohibit impact and righteousness will be marginalized. Corporate America will never change as long as there are no Kingdom citizens **on** the board. The ekklesia fortified with the Holy Spirit must engage economics, finance, healthcare, education, social humanity, entertainment, and sports. ... *The kingdom of heaven is like leaven, which a woman took and hid in three measures of meal till it was all leavened.* MATTHEW 13:33.

Religion will conspire to hide the truth in an effort to impede influence. The ekklesia must guard against the temptation to isolate behind walls in the name of religion, we have to *go in.* ...*And I heard a voice saying unto me, Arise, Peter; slay and eat. But I said, not so, Lord: for nothing common or unclean hath at any time entered into my mouth. But the voice answered me again from heaven, what God hath cleansed, that call not thou common.* ACTS 11:7-9. We must guard against the temptation to become tribal. When God said ...*let them have dominion... fill the earth and subdue it;* GENESIS 1:26-28, He established His Kingdom Government in the earth. God promised Abraham that he would make his seed a nation, not a religion. *...you shall be a father of many nations...* GENESIS 17:1-4.

Nations don't exist without government. The priority shouldn't be religion but correct government. Man's mistrust of government is not without understanding. Men of our time want to be rulers but they don't want to follow God's pattern. ... *The kings of the earth set themselves, and the rulers take counsel together, against the Lord, and against his anointed, saying, let us break their bands asunder, and cast away their cords from us. He that sitteth in the heavens shall laugh...* PSALM 2:1-5. Because men won't follow God's model the world is filled with dictators, tyrants, despots, and oligarchs. When we fail to engage the earthly government will be left to do as it pleases, with no regard to God's will or God's way. The earthly government will champion ideas that are foreign to God.

I grew up in Pentecostalism. By the time I was 12 years old I could memorize two scriptures, the 23rd Psalms and Acts 2:4. I was baptized and filled with the Holy Ghost on Feb 18, 1971 at the young age of 13. I will never deny that event of my life. I will never regret that day. However, one thing is certain, I need more than one experience to sustain my living. I live each day under the influence of the Holy Spirit. He is more than a thrill to me. Under His influence I have maintained a life of prayer. I try to follow Jesus' model for prayer; *...He went out, and departed into a solitary place, and there He prayed.* MARK1:35. Praying is most probably the one activity that Jesus did more than anything else. Under His influence I have tried to be a good husband. Under His influence I have tried to be a good father. Under His influence I have managed my finances. I believe that the Holy Spirit, misunderstood, has been reduced to a product to be sold to men who have a constant need to be mesmerized and thrilled. The Holy Spirit is more than a moral babysitter. Men aren't looking for a place to worship they are looking for religious theme sanctuaries. It has become fashionable to come to catch a thrill on the holy-ghoster. We need to have a better respect and a better understanding of The Holy Ghost and His influence. *...He breathed on them, and said to them, Receive the Holy Spirit.* JOHN 20:22.

We are the Ekklesia who can turn the community upside down. Fortified and empowered, the Ekklesia will take the earth for the king, impacting it with the king's culture, the king's nature, and the king's will. *However, when He, the Spirit of truth, has come, He will guide you into all truth; for He will not speak on His own authority, but whatever He hears He will speak; and He will tell you things to come. He will glorify Me, for He will take of what is Mine and declare it to you. All things that the Father has are Mine. Therefore, I said that He will take of Mine and declare it to you.* JOHN 16:13-15 *...But if I cast out demons with the finger of God, surely the kingdom of God has come upon you.* LUKE 11:20

In the Genesis story as the earth was created, the earth was without form, it was empty, and it was without light. Then the Spirit of God moved and everything changed. In the Acts 2:4 record there was a sound of a mighty wind. The *ekklesia* that Jesus had commissioned was fortified with the Spirit of God and began to change the world. Whether you are a student of the Old Testament or a charismatic with both feet in the New

Testament, it will be very difficult to deny the kingdom influence of the Holy Spirit. We need to have a better respect and a better understanding of The Holy Spirit and His influence. I pray that you are empowered with this knowledge, as a citizen of the Kingdom of God, fortified with the Holy Spirit you will bring kingdom influence to the community, the university, the home, and the nation.

# Kingdom Priority

## Under Pursuit

☐MATTHEW 6:25-33

*A*nd *he said unto them, I must preach the kingdom of God to other cities also: for therefore am I sent.* LUKE 4:43.

*"seek first the kingdom of God and His righteousness, and all these things shall be added to you."* MATTHEW 6:33.

Priority will help to discover passion. Passion will help to manifest purpose. Purpose will help to establish correct priority. Identify passion to achieve purpose by establishing correct priority. Let's be clear Jesus understood passion, purpose, and priority. *Now his parents went to Jerusalem every year at the feast of the passover.* LUKE 2:41-49 According to the bible story the parents of Jesus had traveled from Jerusalem to Nazareth a full day's journey before they noticed that they had forgotten Jesus. When they finally found him, they were *"astonished"* to find the twelve-year-old sitting, listening and asking questions with teachers and doctors. Jesus replied to them; *"Why did you seek Me? Did you not know that I must be about My Father's business?"* The reply confused his parents because not only did they forget the child, but they forgot why the child was born. Before we charge his parents with neglect ask yourself where would you had looked for Jesus forgetting why he came. Maybe you would have checked the basketball court, or the arcade studio, or maybe at the track. Jesus wouldn't had been found in such places because Jesus understood his priority.

A parallel event happens at the marriage in Cana of Galilee when Jesus was recruited to rescue the wedding banquet from disaster by his mother; *Jesus saith unto her, Woman, what have I to do with thee? mine hour is not yet come.* JOHN 2:1-9.

As Jesus was able to keep his priority, he was often found doing the most unexpected. It would have been more expected for a rival king to march into Jerusalem on a horse to take territory. *All this was done, that it might be fulfilled which was spoken by the prophet, saying, ... Behold, thy King cometh unto thee, meek, and sitting upon an ass, and a colt the foal of an ass. ... Hosanna to the Son of David: Blessed is he that cometh in the name of the Lord; Hosanna in the highest. And when he was come into Jerusalem, all the city was moved, saying, who is this? And the multitude said, this is Jesus the prophet of Nazareth of Galilee.* MATTHEW 21:4-11. Jesus solemnly enters as a humble King of peace entering the city on a donkey arriving in peace, rather than as a war-waging king on a horse. However, let us be clear Jesus is not "taking territory from Caesar". The priority for Jesus is to *"take back"*, to recover, to retrieve, to redeem the territory and government system that was hijacked in the Genesis story. The priority to redeem and restore the man to get back the hijacked kingdom government system.

Religion and ideologies should never become priority. Governments that are more interested in religion will destroy the territory and the citizens that live in it. James and John, two of Jesus' disciples, wanted the destruction of a Samaritan village because they would not receive Jesus. Jesus response to the spirit of terrorism *... the Son of man is not come to destroy men's lives, but to save them...* LUKE 9:56. Jesus had to once again remind his disciples the purpose and priority of his coming.

Born in democracy and raised in religion and as far back as I can remember I was taught to get a good education, find a good job and provide for my family. My priority was to provide good shelter, good security, and put food on the table. Every morning, millions of Americans fight gridlock traffic, going to jobs they hate, working for people they don't like, getting paid for less than they're worth, which defines the phycology of *"the hierarchy of needs".* The democratic republic teaches that men should pursue individual happiness and personal liberties. Clearly this particular priority is likely to put man at risk. *...every man is tempted, when he is drawn away of his own lust,* JAMES 1:14.

*And the Lord God commanded the man, saying, of every tree of the garden thou may freely eat:* GENESIS 2:16. Adam was never driven by want and while he didn't own anything, he had access to everything. Adam never had to join the rat race or climb the cooperate ladder. There was no need to fight gridlock traffic. Adam had access all of the earth resources, the gold, the precious stone, and the oil. Adam was living large. His living address was a place prepared for him in the presence of God. Adam was created in the image of God, in the likeness of God and fortified with the Spirit of God. Adam was empowered and given dominion by God. God was with Adam and Adam was with God. Adam had everything that we wish we could. However, as time passed the wickedness of man became great in the earth, and every intent of his heart made man lose sight of the priority of God, *dominion over the earth.* After God repented that he made man He executed a plan of mitigation and He gave Noah the same priority mandate he gave Adam, to subdue the earth and have dominion. *So, God blessed Noah and his sons, and said to them: "Be fruitful and multiply, and fill the earth.* GENESIS 9:1

Adam, Noah, and Abraham were able to receive God's mandate to have dominion, *fill the earth, subdue the earth, and have dominion.* The mandate makes religion redundant. *The Lord God planted a garden eastward in Eden, and there He put the man...*GENESIS 2:8. *And the Lord said unto Abram, ... Lift up now thine eyes, and look from the place where thou art northward, and southward, and eastward, and westward: For all the land which thou sees, to thee will I give it, and to thy seed forever.... Arise, walk through the land in the length of it and in the breadth of it; for I will give it unto thee.* GENESIS 13:14-17. The mandate and the priority for mankind has always been dominion, nation, and government. Religion and religious liberties have never been the priority. God uses Abraham to birth the nation, Joseph to preserve the nation, Moses to deliver the nation. God uses Joshua to forge a nation.God uses David to rule the nation. The Apostles came to disciple the nations. Jesus died to redeem and save the nation.

God separates Abram from his country, his culture, and his roots, not a religion, to create a nation; not a religion, ...*Now the Lord had said to Abram: "Get out of your country, from your family and from your father's house to a land that I will show you. I will make you a great nation..."* GENESIS 12:1-2.

The history of Joseph is very interesting. Favor follows Joseph from the pit to Potiphar's house, where dominion catches up. *So it was, from the time that he had made him overseer of his house and all that he had, that the Lord blessed the Egyptian's house for Joseph's sake; and the blessing of the Lord was on all that he had in the house and in the field.* GENESIS 39:1-6 Favor continues to shadow him to the prison, where dominion catches up again, ...*the keeper of the prison committed to Joseph's hand all the prisoners who were in the prison; whatever they did there, it was his doing.* GENESIS 39:21-23. The Egyptians can't find such a man as Joseph and favor follows him to the palace. Where not only has dominion caught up but wealth and influence as well. *Then Pharaoh said to Joseph, "Inasmuch as God has shown you all this, there is no one as discerning and wise as you. You shall be over my house, and all my people shall be ruled according to your word; only in regard to the throne will I be greater than you." And Pharaoh said to Joseph, "See, I have set you over all the land of Egypt.* GENESIS 41:37-45 Joseph is reputed to say that *God caused him to be fruitful in the land of his affliction.* GENESIS 41:50-52. When Moses leads the nation out of Egypt, the nation comes out with great wealth.

Just as a dominion needs a domain, the domain needs a government, and the government needs righteousness, the nation will need wealth, *they shall come out with great substance.* GENESIS 15:13-14. David said it best; *I've never seen the righteous forsaken.* PSALMS 37:25. The age-old debate and the pros and cons of tithing goes on to this day. The anti-tithers versus the pro-tithers. The anti-tithers think that churches use tithing as a ploy to defraud. The pro-tithers believe that tithing is a blessing thing or a prosperity thing. Neither group has a proper understanding of the concept of Kingdom tithing. Tithing is not an Old Testament thing nor is it a New Testament prosperity thing. It is about the distribution of Kingdom resources so that all citizens can enjoy wealth that is common. Tithing is a Kingdom thing. The real truth is, tithing is how the nation manifests wealth. Joseph taught Egypt that even though they had access to great prosperity they were required to bring back part of the harvest. *Bring ye all the tithes into the storehouse, that there may be meat in mine house, and prove me now herewith, saith the Lord of hosts, if I will not open you the windows of heaven, and pour you out a blessing, that there shall not be room enough to receive it.* MALACHI 3:10. If there is no bringing, there will be no pouring. *...And I will rebuke the devourer for your sakes, and he shall not destroy the fruits of your ground; neither shall your vine cast her fruit before the time in the field, saith the Lord of hosts.* MALACHI 3:11. If you keep the correct priority God will not only overtake you with blessings but God will secure the blessings and make them sustainable. So, when Jesus says not to worry, He meant what he said, and you can trust what Jesus said.

As the nation developed God gave Moses these words *"...and you shall be to Me a kingdom of priests and a holy nation.' These are the words which you shall speak to the children of Israel."* EXODUS 19:6. That verse proposed that God wants a government that worships. So, imagine, if you are priest who wear crowns, *a royal priesthood, a holy nation, a peculiar people;* 1 PETER 2:9. The democratic republic teaches separation of church and state to avoid intrusion of government on religion. The religious then attempt to assert Kingdom concepts under the authority of the democracy. However, when God created man and commanded him to *subdue* and *have dominion,* He established His government in the earth. GENESIS 1:26-28. Adam abdicated the authority God gave him and forfeited it to the prince of darkness leaving the control of earth to an illegal, illegitimate, counterfeit kingdom, misdirecting the priority.

Elijah understood the priority for the nation, but the prophet had to deal with Ahab who would not follow the Lord's mandate for the nation. 1 KINGS 16:30-31. The king was particularly influenced by his wife, Jezebel. Jezebel was not faithful to the priority and would not be committed to one God. Elijah was so committed to the nation that he rebuked the disobedient king and shut up the rain. Jezebel, in her anger, put out a hit on Elijah for the execution of the prophets of Baal 1 KINGS 19:2. Still God had Elijah's back, protecting and providing for him from the brook, to Zarephath, to the broom tree, to the cave.

There is one common stich in this pattern for each of these men. Each man established a well precise meticulous, divine priority. That is why all of these things; riches, prosperity, blessings, water, food, and clothes followed these men. *And it shall come to pass, if thou shalt hearken diligently unto the voice of the Lord thy God, to observe and to do all his commandments which I command thee this day, that the Lord thy God will set thee on high above all nations of the earth: And all these blessings shall come on thee, and overtake thee, if thou shalt hearken unto the voice of the Lord thy God.* DEUTERONOMY 28:1-2 *Surely goodness and mercy shall follow me all the days of my life; and I will dwell in the house of the Lord Forever.* PSALM 23:6.

Jesus asks a question: "*why do you worry, what you will eat or what you will drink; or what you will wear?*" This question destroys the theory of hierarchy of needs. *Therefore, take no thought, saying, what shall we eat? or, what shall we drink? or, Wherewithal shall we be clothed? (For after all these things do the Gentiles seek:)* religious people have an alternate set of priorities, *...your heavenly Father knows that ye have need of all these things. But seek ye first the kingdom of God, and his righteousness; and all these things shall be added unto you.* MATTHEW 6:25-33. Jesus asks a good question: *why do you worry?* Why are you so consumed with worry? Why are you losing sleep? Why are you short tempered and edgy?

Jesus was targeted by a schizophrenic system of religion and government. Jesus was increasingly popular with the people living in the territory and the religious were intimidated. The Pharisees, and the Sadducees were losing control in the territory. They are no match for the influence of Jesus on the people and they want to put a stop to it. Jesus had to contend with the clash of two illegitimate systems. The Pharisees and Sadducees needed to protect their religious control while Pilate needed to protect Roman control. They made religion the priority and left the government of the territory to Rome and Pilate. They tried to discredit Jesus but without success. Pilate and the religious had one common ambition, how to get Jesus out of the way.

Jesus understood his passion, his purpose, and his priority. *I must preach the kingdom of God to other cities also: for therefore am I sent.* LUKE 4:43. *And Jesus answered him, saying, it is written, that man shall not live by bread alone.* LUKE 4:4. *Jesus saith unto her, …mine hour is not yet come.* JOHN 2:4. *For the Son of Man did not come to destroy men's lives but to save them…. ".* LUKE 9:51-56.

Identify passion to achieve purpose to establish correct priority; *…seek ye first the kingdom of God, and his righteousness; and all these things shall be added unto you.* MATTHEW 6:25-33. In the context of the Kingdom, God's righteousness is God's law and his will. When a man discovers true, destined, authentic passion he will find it in the will of his Lord. Man will discover as well that he cannot follow God's will without following his righteousness and without the pursuit of righteousness he will not be able to pursue the Kingdom of God, the correct priority.

# Kingdom Voices

One Man, One Cross, Two Voices

▢ LUKE 23:46

A nd when Jesus had cried with a loud voice, he said, Father, into thy hands I commend my spirit: and having said thus, he gave up the ghost. LUKE 23:46.

If we truly believe that Jesus is as much man as he is God, we should expect to hear two voices, the voice of authority and the voice of obedience. The voice of the Son of God and the voice of the Son of Man; ...*a child is born, and a son is given.* ISAIAH 9:6. One day Jesus asked his disciples a question; ...*Whom do men say that I the Son of man am?* MATTHEW 16:13-19. Jesus is typically misunderstood. Jesus is not one of a million gods, he is not a failed prophet, and he is not prince charming. Jesus is neither Clark Kent nor Superman. If we want to understand Jesus better it is a good idea to recognize him by His voice. *My sheep hear my voice, and I know them, and they follow me:* JOHN 10:27

Voices can be heard all the way from Genesis. ...*they heard the voice of the Lord God walking in the garden in the cool of the day: and Adam and his wife hid themselves from the presence of the Lord God amongst the trees of the garden.* GENESIS 3:8. The man, as he heard the voice of God walking, was driven by guilt and shame to hide himself. Subsequently Adam followed a different voice that cost him the presence of God. Abram follows a voice that separated him from his country, his culture, and his roots, to create a nation.

*...Now the Lord had said to Abram: "Get out of your country, ...I will make you a great nation..."* GENESIS 12:1-2 God wouldn't let Ishmael die in the desert, *And God heard the voice of the lad; and the angel of God called to Hagar out of heaven, and said unto her, what aileth thee, Hagar? fear not; for God hath heard the voice of the lad where he is.* GENESIS 21:17. Moses, curious with a burning bush, followed a voice to discover his true destiny. *...God called unto him out of the midst of the bush, and said, Moses, Moses. And he said, here am I.* EXODUS 3:4-10. The suicidal prophet, Elijah, was on the run for his life, *... behold, there came a voice unto him, and said, What doest thou here, Elijah* 1 KINGS 19:9-13.

*Blessed is the man that walketh not in the counsel of the ungodly, nor standeth in the way of sinners, nor sitteth in the seat of the scornful.* PSALMS 1:1-3 Do not under any circumstance follow bad ungodly voices. Be careful never to follow the counsel of the ungodly voices. Regard any ungodly voice with prejudice. Voices have the capacity to build ideologies and philosophies. Keep in mind that voices control narratives and the voice that controls the narrative can control the influence. If you listen and follow the wrong voice your life will come to a screeching halt. Everyone hears voices. Voices can be audible, shrewd, overt, and some are much more subtle. We wait to hear what the voices will tell us. Many of our decisions will depend on which voice we listen to. We wait to hear which person we should marry. We wait to hear what career path we should take. We wait to hear which investment we should make. We will decide on which candidate get the vote depending on which voice we hear.

What Jesus does in new testament Judea is the demonstration of ideas that Adam could have manifested had he never listened to the wrong voice. Adam spoke to creation and whatever Adam called them that was the name thereof. *...the Lord God formed every beast of the field, and every fowl of the air; and brought them unto Adam to see what he would call them: and whatsoever Adam called every living creature that was the name thereof.* GENESIS 2:19. Words are ideas conceived and expressed, from precept to concept. Jesus is the word made flesh, making Jesus the *expressed* idea of God. *In the beginning was the Word, and the Word was with God, and the Word was God. The same was in the beginning with God. All things were made by him; and without him was not anything made that was made.* JOHN 1:1-3

There is a distinction between the two men. Jesus, being the Son of Man and the Son of God, speaks with two voices. It is important to know the voice of obedience and the voice of authority. Adam may have been able to speak to creation. Jesus is able to speak to create.

In the New Testament Jesus is recorded to say: ...*If you had known me, you would have known My Father also; He who has seen me has seen the Father; ...Do you not believe that I am in the Father, and the Father in Me? The words that I speak to you I do not speak on my own authority; but the Father who dwells in me... ...I am in the Father and the Father in Me...* JOHN 14:7-11.

Foolish men will attempt to trap Jesus in a crisis of identity. However, Jesus doesn't suffer nor has he ever suffered with identity crisis. ...*a lawyer, asked him a question, tempting him, and saying, Master, which is the great commandment in the law? Jesus said unto him, thou shalt love the Lord thy God with all thy heart, and with all thy soul, and with all thy mind. This is the first and great commandment. And the second is like unto it, thou shalt love thy neighbor as thyself. On these two commandments hang all the law and the prophets.* MAT 22:35-40. It is just like a lawyer to try to use some form of ambiguous legalese to bring the Son of God's legitimacy into question. The Son of Man is spiritually aware; however, the Son of God is equally socially aware. The theologians and the religious elite try to trip the Son of God up with silly questions regarding His validity. *While the Pharisees were gathered together, Jesus asked them, Saying, what think ye of Christ? Whose son, is he? They say unto him, The Son of David. He saith unto them, how then doth David in spirit call him Lord, saying, The Lord said unto my Lord, sit thou on my right hand, till I make thine enemies thy footstool? If David then call him Lord, how is he his son? And no man was able to answer him a word, neither durst any man from that day forth ask him any more questions.* MAT 22:41-46

The Son of Man and the Son of God are one in the same. We should listen to hear His humanity, compassion, and longsuffering. We should listen to hear his sovereignty, authority, forgiveness and his righteousness. We can also hear and recognize the adoration for His Father. The Father that sent his Son. Jacob sent Joseph to see about his brothers; Jesse sent David to a battle camp to see about his brothers; *...And Israel said to Joseph, "Are not your brothers feeding the flock in Shechem? Come, I will send you to them..."* GENESIS 37:13. *Then Jesse said to his son David, ...run to your brothers at the camp."* 1 SAMUEL 17:17-18. *... when the fullness of the time was come, God sent forth his Son...* GALATIANS 4:4. The Son of God comes vested with authority from his Father, and the Father will validate the Son of Man. *... This is my beloved Son, in whom I am well pleased.* MATTHEW 3:17 *... Thou art my beloved Son, in whom I am well pleased.* MARK 1:11.

Jesus came because his father sent him, *the Word became flesh and dwelt among us, and we beheld His glory, the glory as of the only begotten of the Father, full of grace and truth.* JOHN 1:14. *...Behold, a virgin shall be with child, and shall bring forth a son, and they shall call his name Emmanuel, which being interpreted is, God with us.* MATTHEW 1:23, *God sent forth his Son...* GALATIANS 4:4 *...now the birth of Jesus Christ was on this wise: When as his mother, Mary was espoused to Joseph, before they came together, she was found with child of the Holy Ghost.* MATTHEW 1:18. God secured the birth of His son by the Holy Ghost so that no man could take credit for the birth of Jesus. If the birth of Jesus was different, then His life was different as well. His message and His teaching were different. His death had to be different as well.

If you should ever find yourself in front of a judge found guilty and charged with a crime and a man steps up to exchange places with you, follow the voice of that man. If the man is going to exchange his innocence for your guilt and shame, there is nothing left for you to say. Your excuse, your explanation, your defense will be disregarded. The man has exchanged places with you and now the consequence your guilt will become his experience and He is going to die. This is why the crucifixion experience can never be co-opted. The words that Jesus utters from the cross are born out of His experience and should not be used to echo any homily or human discourse. Jesus has assumed your shame, your dishonor and now your experience. It is all on Him. Jesus is the one doing the suffering and dying, hear His voice.

The birth, the message, and the life of Jesus reflect his humanity, compassion, sovereignty, and authority. The crucifixion was the experience of the Child that was born and the Son that was given. The crucifixion was the experience of one man, dying on one cross, voicing seven sayings, with two voices.

## THE SON OF MAN

1. *Woman, behold thy son! Behold thy mother!* JOHN 19:26-27
2. *Eli, Eli, lama Sabachthani? ... My God, my God, why hast thou forsaken me?* MATTHEW 27:46 -MARK 15:34
3. *I thirst.* JOHN 19:28
4. *It is finished: and he bowed his head, and gave up the ghost.* JOHN 19:30

The Son of Man, the Child, will express his loneliness and He will come to know abandonment and thirst. The voice of the Son of man is an expression of longing and a thirst for something that the man lost. The man did not lose religion, he lost dominion, and he lost the presence of God. Ever since that day man has been trying to get back to that place. When man disobeyed God, he was driven out from the presence of God. Man will have to live with yearning, longing, and thirsting. The Son of Man must experience that same longing, and thirsting. Imagine, the Son of Man remembering his eternity, only to be left on the dark isolated corner of time. *...My God, my God, why hast thou forsaken me?* The Son of Man must experience rejection, yes rejection. That is what happened to Adam in the beginning when the man committed treason. *...He drove out the man; and He placed cherubim at the east of the Garden of Eden, and a flaming sword which turned every way, to* *guard the way to the tree of life.* GENESIS 3:23-25. With the fullness of time, when Jesus is made sin, the Son of Man will feel forsaken.

## THE SON OF GOD

1. *Father, forgive them; for they know not what they do.* LUKE 23:34
2. *Verily I say unto thee, today shalt thou be with me in paradise.* LUKE 23:43
3. *Father, into thy hands I commend my spirit:* LUKE 23:46
4. *It is finished: and he bowed his head, and gave up the ghost.* JOHN 19:30

*Yea, though I walk through the valley of the shadow of death, I will fear no evil: for thou art with me; thy rod and thy staff they comfort me.* PSALMS 23:4 When Adam rebelled against God he was driven from His presence. After God posted a guard to keep the man out Adam could no longer *be with Him.* Adam will have to settle that God will be with him. To know that God will be with you no matter what is good but it is not God's design. We were created to be with Him. He put the man in the garden, He made David lay down in green pastures. And now Jesus is hangin out with a couple of transgressors. One of them has a faith experience and just as he is about to step through the gate, Jesus, the Lord, the Son of God reaches out to the guilty criminal and restores his access. Jesus does this because He, the legitimate Son of God has the authority to redeem. He the Son of God has every right to save this man. The religious elite has spent three years trying to deny the legitimacy of Jesus. Questioning every move of the Son of God. Asking who is he and who does he think he is? Where did he come from? He came from the Father, and the Son of God is within his sovereign right to redeem the man from eternal destruction.

Remember the Son comes from the Father. *The words that I speak to you I do not speak on my own authority; but the Father who dwells in me...* JOHN 14:7-11. When we hear the voice of the Son, we know that he speaks with the voice of authority. He is the Christ, the son of the Living God. Now ask yourself this question; how is the Son of Man who knew no sin going to die? Remember, the consequence of sin is death. Therefore, the man who knew no sin will not come to death. As a matter of fact, death has no claim to Jesus. *...He made Him who knew no sin to be sin for us, that we might become the righteousness of God in Him.* 2 CORINTHIANS 5:21. Not until God counts Jesus among the transgressors will death be able to assert any right. *He poured out His soul unto death, And He was numbered with the transgressors, and He bore the sin of many, and made intercession for the transgressors.* ISAIAH 53:12. *...And He was numbered with the transgressors...* LUKE 22:37. The word *poured* is an active verb, meaning that Jesus doesn't just wait for life to fade. Rather He is *going* to die and death will not approach until Jesus gives the word. Jesus doesn't languish, He is going to die. If no man can receive credit for the conception or birth of Jesus then no man can be charged with his death. I am hesitant to call Jesus my hero because heroes put their lives at risk. Jesus didn't risk his life he gave his life. To call Jesus a hero diminishes his death. A hero will take a risk, the savior will give his life. When we say, Jesus died for us, do we clearly understand the expression? Jesus did not succumb; death will have to wait for the voice of the Son to give up the ghost. *Father, into thy hands I commend my spirit: ...I lay down my life, that I might take it again. No man taketh it from me, but I lay it down of myself. I have authority to lay it down, and I have authority to take it again. This commandment have I received of my Father.* JOHN 10:17-18.

*And when Jesus had cried with a loud voice, he said, Father, into thy hands I commend my spirit: and having said thus, he gave up the ghost.* LUKE 23:46.

# Kingdom Fortified

Safeguard Security Safety Shelter Sanctuary

☐PSALMS 91:1-6

H e who dwells in the secret place of the Most High shall abide under the shadow of the Almighty. I will say of the Lord, "He is my refuge and my fortress; My God, in Him I will trust." Surely, He shall deliver you from the snare of the fowler and from the perilous pestilence. He shall cover you with His feathers, and under His wings you shall take refuge; His truth shall be your shield and buckler. You shall not be afraid of the terror by night, nor of the arrow that flies by day, nor of the pestilence that walks in darkness, nor of the destruction that lay waste at noonday. PSALMS 91:1-6

We are currently experiencing very turbulent times. The citizens of the republic face social and racial injustice. Expressions of dissent are manifested in civil disobedience and violent political insurrection. Law enforcement agencies are faced with gun violence and behavior that is predatory. Despair, panic, and fear lead the media headlines. Many have suffered loss of loved-ones, property, and secured well-being. COVID has influenced the culture and men who were created to be social beings are afraid to visit friends and family. The citizens are losing faith and trust in government leadership. Many of the political leaders suffer from a lack of integrity. It would seem that every man is for himself. The citizens need someone to restore security, safety, protection, and well-being. This writing has come to encourage all of us that we can be fortified in the Kingdom of God. The poor in spirit, the mournful, the meek, the merciful, peacemakers, and the persecuted will be blessed in the secured fortified presence of the Kingdom. Those who thirst and hunger after righteousness will find justice in the fortified sanctuary of the Kingdom.

Man was created in the image and the likeness of the invisible God who fortified man with His Spirit, *...breathed into his nostrils the breath of life; and man became a living soul.* GENESIS 2:7. After the man became a living soul, he was placed in the presence of the invisible God. *The Lord God planted a garden eastward in Eden, and there He put the man whom He had formed.* GENESIS 2:8. *God blessed them...* GENESIS 1:26-28. Imagine that our covenant with God has at least one addendum. The addendum stipulates that as long as man is obedient, he can enjoy the fortified presence of God. Man's obedience will obligate God's continued protection. So, from the very beginning as long as the man remained where God put him, in His presence, the fortified man would be secured. The very presence of the King will protect the citizens from all foreign enemies. Only when man, through rebellion or disobedience, leaves the presence of God will man become an exposed target. *Because thou hast made the LORD, which is my refuge, even the Most High, thy habitation; There shall no evil befall thee, neither shall any plague come nigh thy dwelling. For he shall give his angels charge over thee, to keep thee in all thy ways. ...Thou shalt tread upon the lion and adder: the young lion and the dragon shalt thou trample under feet.* PSALMS 91:9-13. I am convinced that if we stay where God put us, we can be secure and fortified. Man is a living soul spiritually, physically, and mentally fortified.

God created beings. God did not build robots. He created heavenly angelic beings and earthly human beings. The beings can choose to obey and worship. Robots can only follow instructions coded for them. *I call heaven and earth to record this day against you, that I have set before you, life and death, blessing and cursing: therefore, choose life, that both thou and thy seed may live:* DEUTERONOMY 30:19.

We know that the human being was given the capacity to choose. Therefore, man can choose obedience, devotion, and worship. However, one day an angelic being chose to rebel and that heavenly being was cast down to the earth, where he became a deceiver and predator. If Adam was sought out and deceived by this predator to hijack the world systems you are potential prey for the same predator. You, man, need to be fortified. The predator still roams about the earth going to and fro, up and down seeking whom he may devour. *Now there was a day when the sons of God came to present themselves before the LORD, and Satan came also among them. And the LORD said unto Satan, Whence comest thou? Then Satan answered the LORD, and said, from going to and fro in the earth, and from walking up and down in it.* JOB 1:6-7. In the preceding text *sons of God* is a reference to angelic beings. Satan complained that God had Job under fortified protective custody. *Hast not thou made a hedge about him, and about his house, and about all that he hath on every side? thou hast blessed the work of his hands, and his substance is increased in the land.* JOB 1:10. Your continued prosperity, success and well-being is dependent on the fortified presence of God.

When Adam declared independence and committed an act of treason and disobedience, he forfeited the fortified presence of God. God had to build a wall because man couldn't be trusted to respect God's righteousness. *So, he drove out the man; and he placed at the east of the garden of Eden Cherubims, and a flaming sword which turned every way, to keep the way of the tree of life.* GENESIS 3:24. Adam was the first victim of identity theft and the governing system was hijacked by the prince of darkness. Adam abdicated authority invested in him and forfeited it to the *prince of darkness,* he left the control of the world to an illegal, illegitimate, counterfeit control. The rebel in chief proceeded to establish his illegitimate regime, asserting illegal and counterfeit control of the world systems. As time passed the wickedness of man became great in the earth, and every intent of his heart made man lose sight of the priority of God, *dominion over the earth*. Man lost his fortified protection in God.

The bible tells the story of a man of God sent by the word of the Lord to Jeroboam in Bethel. When the King stretched out his hand against the man of God, the King's hand was shriveled up. The King asked the man of God to pray for his hand. When the King's hand was restored the King offered a reward. However, the man of God was given special instructions. *...it charged me by the word of the Lord, saying, eat no bread, nor drink water, nor turn again by the same way that thou came. So, he went another way, and returned not by the way that he came to Bethel.* 1 KINGS 13:8-10. However, an older prophet, a predator motivated by a culture of deception tempted the man of God to contravene divine instructions. *...He said unto him, I am a prophet also as thou art; and an angel spoke unto me by the word of the Lord, saying, bring him back with thee into thine house, that he may eat bread and drink water. But he lied unto him.* 1 KINGS 13:11-24. You will lose fortified spiritual protection if you follow the counsel of the ungodly. Never expect godly consequences if you follow ungodly direction. *And when he was gone, a lion met him by the way, and slew him: and his carcass was cast in the way, and the ass stood by it, the lion also stood by the carcass.* 1 KINGS 13:24. Without divine protection you can end up a carcass on the side of the road, with a lion standing by, licking his paws.

The Heavenly Host mentioned in the Bible refers to the army of angels. The Heavenly Host is responsible for the security of both Heaven and Earth. The Host will provide protection and safety. The Host will fortify the territory and the gates of hell will not prevail. There are stories in the bible that tell of the work of the Host. The very first mention of them is in Genesis *...Jacob went on his way, and the angels of God met him. And when Jacob saw them, he said, this is God's host:* GENESIS 32:1-2. It is the responsibility of the host to protect creation tranquility, well-being, and security of the territory. They are the fortified infrastructure that protects from all enemies imagined, animal, mineral, vegetable, biological, or human, foreign or domestic.

Established in the United States are dozens of federal law enforcement agencies under the executive departments, as well as the legislative and judicial branches of the federal government. All of these agencies were established to protect and defend the citizens and the territory. Without them the territory would be left to the mercies of predators and enemies, domestic and foreign. FEMA will come to reassure us when disaster strikes.

The agency's primary purpose is to coordinate the response to a disaster that has occurred that overwhelms the resources of local and state authorities. CBP is the largest federal law enforcement agency of the Department of Homeland Security and is the country's primary border control organization. The FBI is the domestic intelligence and security service of the United States and its principal federal law enforcement agency. A leader in counter-terrorism, counterintelligence, and criminal investigative organization, the FBI has jurisdiction over violations of more than 200 categories of federal crimes. The DEA is the law enforcement agency tasked with combating drug trafficking and distribution within the U.S. NIH is the primary agency responsible for the security of biomedical research and public health. The CDC is the agency charged with the protection of public health and safety through the control and prevention of disease, injury, and disability. The CDC especially focuses its attention on infectious disease, food borne pathogens, environmental health, occupational safety and health, health promotion, and injury prevention designed to improve the health of the citizens. The CDC also conducts research and provides information on non-infectious diseases, such as obesity and diabetes.

All these agencies share the responsibilities for the domestic tranquility, well-being, and security of the territory. They are the fortified infrastructure that protects from all enemies foreign or domestic. If kings, emperors, sovereigns, and republics know the value of fortified security how much more does God know to fortify.

Now consider the deployed Kingdom Heavenly Host of God. *...when Joshua was by Jericho, that he lifted up his eyes and looked, and behold, there stood a man over against him with his sword drawn in his hand: and Joshua went unto him, and said unto him, Art thou for us, or for our adversaries? And he said, Nay; but as captain of the host of the Lord, am I now come.* JOSHUA 5:13-15. Joshua saw a dude bigger than life with his sword drawn, prepared to fight. At one command the captain of the host will fight to secure the victory for the nation.

There are further reports that the Host can be stealthy. *And when the servant of the man of God arose early and went out, there was an army, surrounding the city with horses and chariots. And his servant said to him, Alas, my master! What shall we do? So, he answered, do not fear, for those who are with us are more than those who are with them. And Elisha prayed, and said, Lord, I pray, open his eyes that he may see. Then the Lord opened the eyes of the young man, and he saw. And behold, the mountain was full of horses and chariots of fire all around Elisha.* 2 KINGS 6:15-17. There are days when it seems that our enemies will defeat and destroy us. However, I will agree with the prophet Elisha that even when we can't see them, the Host is present and ready to fight. Remember Jesus has said that the gates of hell shall not prevail.

Not only will God protect and fortify the citizen. God will protect our substance as well. *...I will rebuke the devourer for your sakes, and he shall not destroy the fruits of your ground; neither shall your vine cast her fruit before the time in the field, saith the Lord of hosts.* MALACHI 3:10-12. Tithing is about the distribution of Kingdom resources. Bringing the tithe is much more than an investment it is also the system to protect and secure the wealth of the Kingdom. Creation is always producing. GENESIS 1:11-24. The earth was designed to produce, even so, part of the design is to never exhaust all of the resources. Have you ever heard of a broke government expanding? Is it possible for a kingdom to have glory and no resources or wealth? It is highly unlikely that any government could increase territory without wealth. So, God gave Adam access to the resources of the earth. It was never God's intent that His government should ever be broke or without resources. Man received the mandate, *...be fruitful and multiply; ...replenish the earth, ...fill the earth and subdue it.* Man does not have the right to exploit or deplete resources.

Notice an old testament pattern; from Abraham to Isaac to Joseph the level of substance increases. Abram goes to Egypt with substance but when he leaves, he is very rich, GENESIS 12:10–20. When Isaac leaves Gerar he isn't just prosperous he has become very prosperous. GENESIS 26:12–14. After everything Joseph experienced, from the pit all the way to the palace God has caused him to be fruitful. Remember what God said to Abraham…*Know of a surety…afterward shall they come out with great substance.* GENESIS 15:13–14. As long as we are obedient to God not even famine can devourer our substance.

We should join the children of Israel to sing a song unto the Lord, saying that he has triumphed gloriously. We will sing that the Lord is our strength and he has fortified us. The Lord is our salvation and we will prepare for him a habitation. Let us declare the Lord as a man of war. Our enemies will stumble and fall, they will sink to the bottom like a stone. Our enemies will pursue us to overtake us. Our enemies' lust will only be satisfied when they divide the spoil. However, our Lord will rebuke the devourer for us. The Lord has redeemed us and planted us in his secured fortified sanctuary. EXODUS 15:1-17.

Jesus declared that the poor in spirit, the mournful, the meek, the merciful, peacemakers, and the persecuted will be blessed in the His secured fortified presence. Those who thirst and hunger after righteousness will find justice in the fortified sanctuary. MATTHEW 5:2-10.

We can testify with David; *The Lord is my light and my salvation; whom shall I fear? the Lord is the strength of my life; of whom shall I be afraid? When the wicked, even mine enemies and my foes, came upon me to eat up my flesh, they stumbled and fell.* PSALMS 27:1-2. As citizens of the Kingdom, we will not be intimidated. We will not run and hide out in caves; we will step up. We have been authorized and commissioned to stomp on the enemy's head *…Behold, I give unto you power to tread on serpents and scorpions, and over all the power of the enemy: and nothing shall by any means hurt you.* LUKE 10:18-19

# Kingdom Treasured Pearl

## A Treasure Pearl Value: Priceless

T*he kingdom of heaven is like treasure hidden in a field, which a man found and hid; and for joy over it he goes and sells all that he has and buys that field.* MATTHEW 13:44. The hidden treasure is secured under sovereign ownership. The man could only buy the field giving him access to the treasure but not ownership. Man was given dominion over everything on the earth. He was given access to all things on the earth as well; however, he could never assert ownership; *...the Lord God commanded the man, saying, of every tree of the garden thou may freely eat: ...but of the fruit of the tree which is in the midst of the garden, God hath said, Ye shall not eat of it, neither shall ye touch it, lest ye die.* GENESIS 2:16; 3:2-3. At the discretion of the sovereign owner, the man will learn the light, the truth, and the knowledge regarding the value of the treasure. *...we speak the wisdom of God in a mystery, even the hidden wisdom, which God ordained before the world unto our glory: Which none of the princes of this world knew: for had they known it, they would not have crucified the Lord of glory. ...But God hath revealed them unto us by his Spirit: for the Spirit searches all things, yea, the deep things of God. For what man knoweth the things of a man, save the spirit of man which is in him? even so the things of God knoweth no man, but the Spirit of God.* 1 CORINTHIANS 2:7-11

Satan is called the prince of darkness for a reason. Satan would like nothing more than to keep man in the dark, it is his ambition to keep man from this treasure. *The god of this world hath blinded the minds of them which believe not, lest the light of the glorious gospel of Christ, who is the image of God, should shine unto them.* 2 CORINTHIANS 4:2. The antagonist pulls levers and pushes buttons hiding behind the curtain of smoke, fire, and religion to keep man from his true identity and destiny. The enemy wants to keep us obsessed with the failure of disobedient man that we lose sight and knowledge of the man that God created. *The sower soweth the word. And these are they by the way side, where the word is sown; but when they have heard, Satan cometh immediately, and taketh away the word that was sown in their hearts.* MARK 4:14. There are some simple truths the god of this world wants to hide from you. Men will gladly give up everything they own to come to the kingdom. Men will trade wickedness, iniquity, corruption and debauchery for the true value of the treasure. Men will gladly trade depression, disillusion, disease, and sickness for the treasure. The man in the parable didn't stop until he gained unlimited, unfettered access to the treasure. Religion is dangerous because religion thrives with illegitimate governments to keep man from the treasure. Their lack of integrity sets up environments that are given to exploitation, despotism, and injustice. By their nature oppressors are psychotic and paranoid and they are driven by fear and insecurity. When the psychosis advances to delusion the men who tell lies begin to believe the lies the men tell.

Remember the cliché, *"a diamond in the rough."* Remember that when you discover the hidden treasure that it may not look like the treasure you were expecting. What Joseph could see in the pit was not what Joseph saw in his dream. Until Moses discovered that he was not the prince of Egypt but rather the son of slaves he was not able to manifest his true destiny. It is quite possible to uncover the hidden treasure in the most unlikely place. The value and the abundance of the treasure will be certified and determined by the owner who buried it, not by the need of the discoverer who unearthed it. The Antithesis of Jesus brings added value to the treasure. To pursue the Kingdom of God and His righteousness, we need the mind of Christ. *Think not that I am come to destroy the law, or the prophets: I am not come to destroy, but to fulfil.* MATTHEW 5:17.

Who better to teach, demonstrate, and help us to understand His righteousness than Jesus himself?

*Again, the kingdom of heaven is like unto a merchant man, seeking goodly pearls: who, when he had found one pearl of great price, went and sold all that he had, and bought it.* MATTHEW 13:45. The Kingdom of God is the pearl by which all human inspired dominions must be measured. Jesus never taught religion. Jesus spent three years teaching his disciples about the virtues of the Kingdom of Heaven and demonstrated how the government of His kingdom works. Jesus came to redeem man and to re-establish His Kingdom. To say that Jesus established a religion is to diminish and categorized the Son of God, putting him on the same level as all other religious ideologues. Religions of the world are established and developed by men with ideas about God. *In the beginning was the Word, and the Word was with God, and the Word was God. The same was in the beginning with God. All things were made by him; and without him was not anything made that was made.* JOHN 1:1-3. Jesus didn't come to the earth with ideas about God. Jesus is the expressed idea of God walking on two legs. Jesus is not a religion. Jesus is the idea of God in the flesh.

In freshwater rivers and ponds, mussels produce pearls, while in saltwater, they are made by oysters. Clams and mussels can be in fresh or saltwater, but oysters are found only in salt or brackish habitats. Clams burrow into the soft sediment, where they hide in the mud or sand. In the darkness of the mud and sand deep in the sea is where the pearl is created. However, the brilliance of the pearl will only be revealed in light, bringing added value to the Kingdom. As we seek the Kingdom of God, we learn kingdom influence, culture, righteousness, peace, and joy. We are encouraged by Jesus to actively track down, pursue, long for, desire the Kingdom of God. To seek is not a random activity. The value of the treasure will be revealed at the discretion of the sovereign owner. The value of the pearl can only be known as the pearl is expose to light. It is not enough just to know the

Kingdom of God; we need to understand the righteousness of God as well. The devil is not called the prince of darkness because he lurks in the night. *The god of this world hath blinded the minds of them which believe not, lest the light of the glorious gospel of Christ, who is the image of God, should shine unto them.* 2 CORINTHIANS 4:2.

As Jesus shares the truths regarding treasures and pearls you will discover that there are differences between the two. First treasures are meant to be buried, that is why you have to "seek" the Kingdom. The discovery of Kingdom value will not be unearthed casually or passively. The truths of the treasure are revealed at the discretion of the owner. *Henceforth I call you not servants; for the servant knoweth not what his lord doeth: but I have called you friends; for all things that I have heard of my Father I have made known unto you.* JOHN 15:15. Remember the domain is the sovereign property belonging to the King, *the earth is the Lord's.* We must actively pursue the Kingdom. The man never tried to carry the treasure away nor did he try to assert ownership. Rather, the man procured the field to gain access to the treasure. *...the Lord God commanded the man, saying, of every tree of the garden thou may freely eat:* GENESIS 2:16. Capitalism teaches that private ownership brings profit and value. The Kingdom teaches that fruitfulness and increased value comes from access. While Adam didn't own anything, he had access to everything. The rivers, the trees yielding fruit with seed. The beast and cattle, meat to eat. Adam had access to the gold, the precious stone, and the oil. The man was not created to exploit, abuse, waste, or destroy any resources for his own enrichment. Democracies, autocracies, plutocracies and capitalisms work to assert human ownership destroying access. The term ownership doesn't apply to property only. The Lord owns the wealth, the influence, the authority, the wisdom, and the victories. It is God who has gotten us the victory. *...he hath done marvelous things: his right hand, and his holy arm, hath gotten him the victory...* PSALMS 98:1-3. God can say, *...it is he that giveth thee power to get wealth...* DEUTERONOMY 8:18. The treasure brings value to the Kingdom as it is discovered; *for all things that I have heard of my Father I have made known unto you.* JOHN 15:15.

The pearl brings value to the Kingdom as it is exposed to light demonstrating its brilliance. *In him was life; and the life was the light of men. And the light shineth in darkness; and the darkness comprehended it not ... The same came for a witness, to bear witness of the Light, that all men through him might believe.* JOHN 1:1-7. This testimony is from the school of psychology. This is why Jesus tells us to *"repent"*. Jesus instructs us to change our way of thinking. He is the witness of the Light that we should receive so we may walk in the knowledge of our true purpose and destiny. His *light* gives us full and complete understanding of His righteousness and His life. *...we have received, not the spirit of the world, but the spirit which is of God; that we might know the things that are freely given to us of God. ...For who hath known the mind of the Lord, that he may instruct him? But we have the mind of Christ.* 1 CORINTHIANS 2:10. Jesus made the announcement; *Repent, for the kingdom of heaven is at hand* MATTHEW 4:17.

David said it well *...I am fearfully and wonderfully made: ...Thine eyes did see my substance, yet being unperfect; and in thy book all my members were written, which in continuance were fashioned... How precious also are thy thoughts unto me, O God! how great is the sum of them! If I should count them, they are more in number than the sand: when I awake, I am still with thee.* PSALMS 139:13-18. *...God saw everything that he had made, and, behold, it was very good.* GENESIS 1:31.